TALBOTT SPRINGS ELEMENTARY SCHOOL

FRONTIERLAND

INQUIRING ABOUT

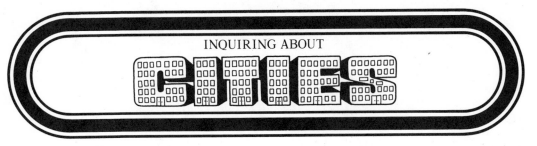

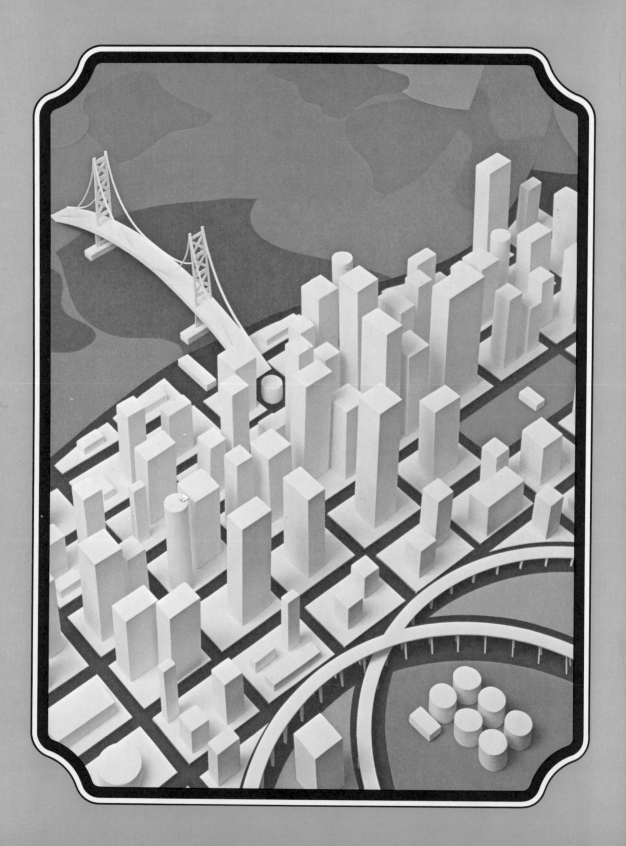

HOLT **Databank** SYSTEM

A SOCIAL SCIENCE PROGRAM

William R. Fielder, General Editor

INQUIRING ABOUT

STUDIES IN GEOGRAPHY AND ECONOMICS

William R. Fielder

Professor and Director
Division of Graduate Studies in Education
Oregon State University
Corvallis, Oregon

Georgiana Feeney

Former Professor of Human Development
Pacific Oaks College
Pasadena, California

Holt, Rinehart and Winston, Publishers

NEW YORK   TORONTO   LONDON   SYDNEY

Professor William R. Fielder, the General Editor of the HOLT DATABANK SYS-TEM, received his Ed.D. in Elementary Education from Stanford University in 1960. Prior to his present position as Professor and Director, Division of Graduate Studies in Education, Oregon State University, he served on the faculties of San Jose State College, Stanford University, Michigan State University, and The Claremont Graduate School and University Center. He has acted as director of a number of educational research projects, including projects in differentiated staffing and instructional television, and has also served as a consultant to local and regional school systems. Professor Fielder is a co-author of *Social Study: Inquiry in Elementary Classrooms* (1966) and a contributor to a variety of professional journals.

Dr. Georgiana Feeney, co-author of *Inquiring About Cities*, was Professor of Human Development at Pacific Oaks College. Prior to her last position, Dr. Feeney was Assistant Professor of Human Relations and Director of the Mary B. Eyre Children's School at Scripp's College. She also served on the faculty of the Claremont Graduate School.

ACKNOWLEDGMENTS

For the map on page 192, the authors extend grateful acknowledgment to the Hershey Foods Corporation for permission to use the Hershey trademark;

For the art on pages 215 and 216, for permission to adapt material from *Urban Design: The Architecture of Towns and Cities* by Paul D. Spreiregen. Copyright © 1965 by the American Institute of Architects. Used with permission of McGraw-Hill Book Company.

COVER ILLUSTRATION by Marvin Goldman.

Credits for text photographs and art appear on pages 309–310.

Printed in the United States of America
ISBN: 0-03-089784-X

79 071 98765

Contents

1 CITY LIFE   1

The Beat of the City   2

2 WERE THESE CITIES?   19

Circle and Cross   20

THE CROSS   21
THE CIRCLE   24

Circleville   27

FOUR MAPS FOR CIRCLEVILLE   30
WAS THIS A CITY?   32

Tikal: Where Is There?   35

THE TEMPLE OF THE GIANT JAGUAR   38
MESSAGES EVERYWHERE   42
GROWING UP IN TIKAL   49
WHEN TIME STOPPED   54

Zimbabwe: Where Is There?   58

GRASS AND ROCKS   59
RUINS OF STONE   60
THE STORY OF THE WALLS   62
THE STORY OF THE PEOPLE   65
THE STORY OF ZIMBABWE HILL   67

Mohenjo-daro: Where Is There?   70

TREASURES IN THE MUD   73
LIFE IN MOHENJO-DARO   76
HOW DID IT END?   82

3 WHERE ON EARTH? 83

A Caravan in Cairo 84

STEPPE AND DESERT 88
TIMBUKTU 92

Cities on the Land 95

CITY SITES 96
LONDON 98

Rivers, Oceans, and Land 100

RIVER'S EDGE 101
OCEAN'S EDGE 103
LAND'S EDGE 106

Denver 108

GOLD RUSH 108
AFTER THE GOLD RUSH 112

Chicago 116

MOVING WEST 116
MUDDY STREETS 117
A MIGHTY CITY 119

New York 123

THE ISLAND WILL SINK! 123
A WORLD OF WATER 125

4 CITIES FROM THE INSIDE OUT 129

Like Doughnuts and Targets 130

EXPLAINING BY PRETENDING 130
THE HOLE IN THE DOUGHNUT 133

All About the C.B.D.   135

THE C.B.D. LONG AGO   135
STREETCARS CHANGED THE C.B.D.   138
HOW THE C.B.D. CHANGED   141
SKYSCRAPERS CHANGED THE C.B.D.   142
ELECTRIC ELEVATORS CHANGED THE C.B.D.   144
THE C.B.D. TODAY   146

Population and Density   148

POPULATION IS A NUMBER   149
DENSITY IS A NUMBER AND SPACE   150
THEY ARE NOT THE SAME   151

Three City Families   152

THE RAMOS FAMILY   154
THE STEIN FAMILY   158
THE MAGEE FAMILY   162
CITIES FROM THE INSIDE OUT   166

5   WHERE ARE THE EDGES?   167

Last Ring Around the City   168

ONE MORE RING   168
HINTERLANDS ARE SPECIAL   170

Mapping the Hinterlands   172

GREATVILLE AND WORLDTOWN   173
LOOKING FOR OTHER CLUES   174

Hinterlands, U.S.A.   179

BANGOR, MAINE   180
ATLANTA, GEORGIA   182
OMAHA, NEBRASKA   184
LOS ANGELES, CALIFORNIA   186
HONOLULU, HAWAII   188
NOME, ALASKA   190

Cities Without Edges 192

CHOCOLATE TOWN 192
MEGALOPOLIS 193

6 TIN LIZZIE 195

Just Imagine! 196
Mr. Fixit 199
Horseless Carriages 202
The Model T 207

FORD'S ASSEMBLY LINE 210
TIN LIZZIE 212

Cars Changed the City 214

HOW ST. LOUIS CHANGED 215
SPACE FOR PARKING 217
SPACE FOR MOVING 220

7 RIVER AND CLOUD 223

Water 224

DROP IN THE BUCKET 224
CITY WATER 228

Down the Drain 232

CAN A LAKE DIE? 232
CAN A RIVER DIE? 236
CAN A RIVER COME BACK TO LIFE? 238

Air 242

DIVE IN! 242
CLEANING THE AIR OCEAN 242

The Tulsa Mystery 244

FACTS ABOUT TULSA 245
CLUES TO THE MYSTERY 248

The La Porte Mystery   250

IS THE MYSTERY REAL?   251
A SCIENTIFIC ANSWER   253

Trapped   256

SMOGIGATED   256
WHO DID IT?   259

How to Mine a City   263

MINES IN THE CITY   264
THE HISTORY OF THIS PAGE   266
BICYCLE, TRICYCLE, RECYCLE   269

8   CITY PLANNING   271

People and Their Cities   272

A CLOSER LOOK   273

Old Planned Cities   275

BUILT IN A HUNDRED DAYS   276
UNDER PENN'S HAT   279
THE NATION'S CAPITAL   283

A City Mix   286

HOW TO MIX A CITY   287
A LITTLE BIT OF EVERYTHING   292

Your Children's Cities   293

Glossary   296

Index   302

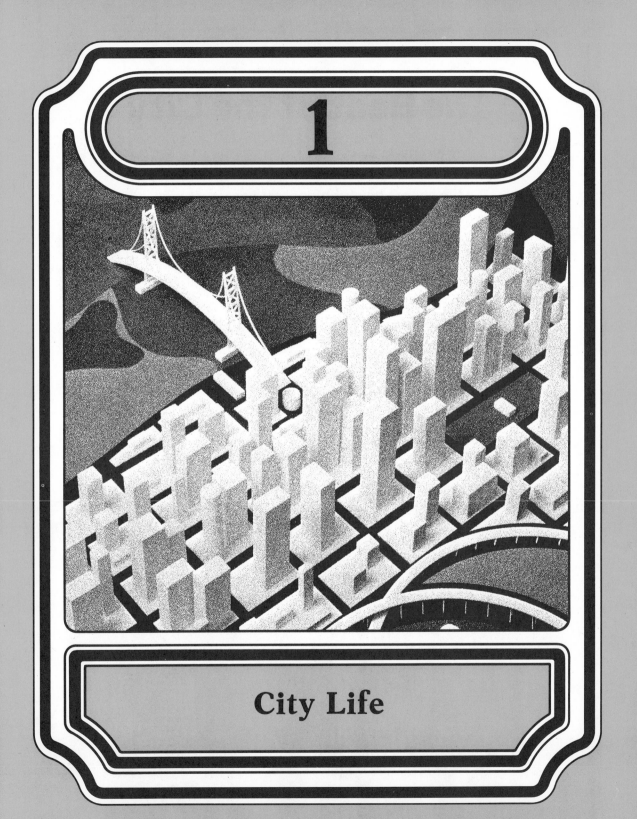

1

City Life

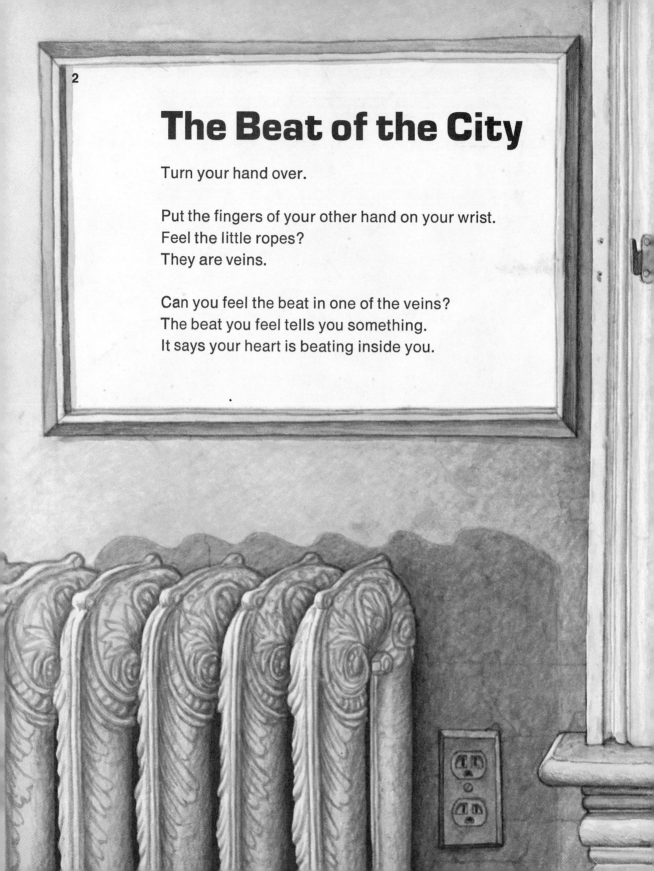

The Beat of the City

Turn your hand over.

Put the fingers of your other hand on your wrist.
Feel the little ropes?
They are veins.

Can you feel the beat in one of the veins?
The beat you feel tells you something.
It says your heart is beating inside you.

4

You have seen pictures of cities.
You know cities are big, crowded places.

Cities were big, even long ago.

Cities are growing all the time.
They get bigger and bigger.
Now cities are giants.

You are learning
about cities.
You will try
to feel
the beat
of these giants.

You will use
your eyes
and your ears.
You will use
your brains
and your bodies.
You will try
to feel
the beat,
beat,
beat
of the city.

Try to feel
the beat
of these giants.
Try to feel
the beat,
beat,
beat
of the city.

Use
your eyes
and your ears.
Use
your brains
and your bodies.
Feel
the beat.

City streets are filled with cars and trucks.
The cars and trucks are never still.
They are part of the beat of the city.

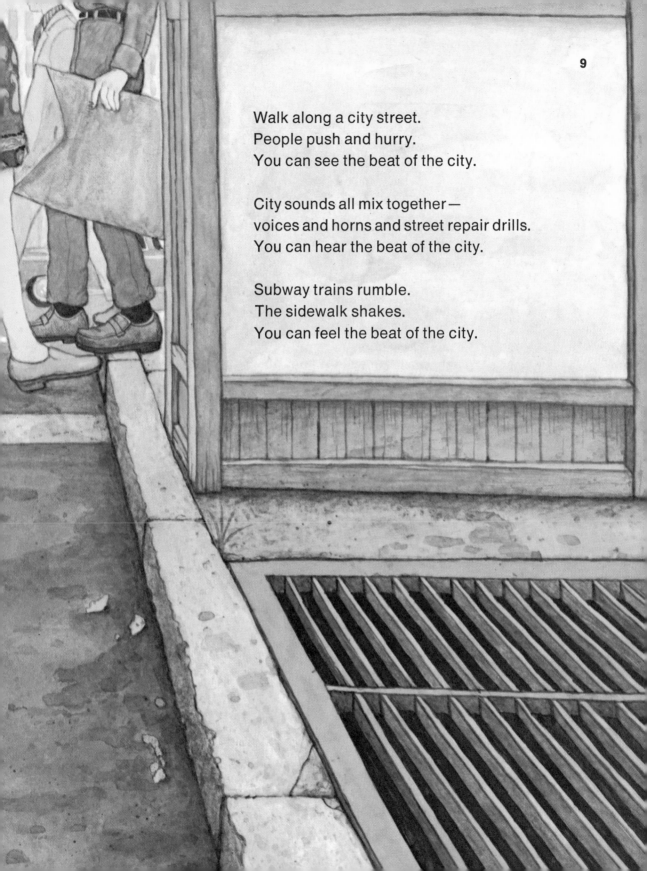

Walk along a city street.
People push and hurry.
You can see the beat of the city.

City sounds all mix together—
voices and horns and street repair drills.
You can hear the beat of the city.

Subway trains rumble.
The sidewalk shakes.
You can feel the beat of the city.

Think of city sights.
Lights blink and flash.
Everything moves in a hurry.

When it rains, umbrellas bump.
Taxis speed by.
Buses are full.
Cars skid.
Can you hear their brakes?

SALE
10%
OFF

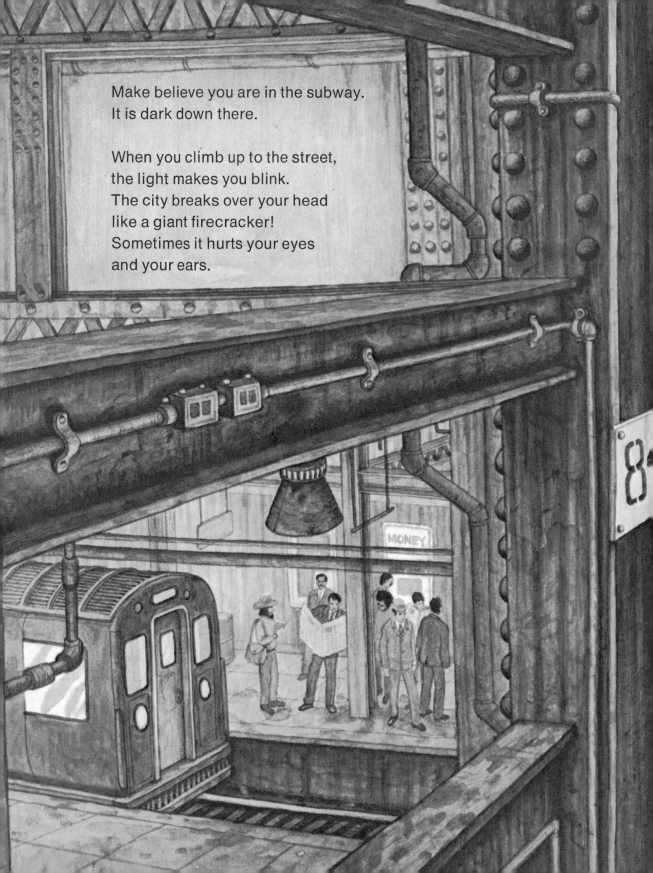

Make believe you are in the subway.
It is dark down there.

When you climb up to the street,
the light makes you blink.
The city breaks over your head
like a giant firecracker!
Sometimes it hurts your eyes
and your ears.

84 TH ST.

But then you push your way into the crowd.
You are part of the city, too.
You feel
its beat,
beat,
beat.

14

When you were little, did you ever move
from one home to another?
In the daytime, it was exciting.
You thought about making new friends.
You liked exploring new places.

But in bed at night, you missed your best friend.
You missed your old house.
You wished you could move back again!

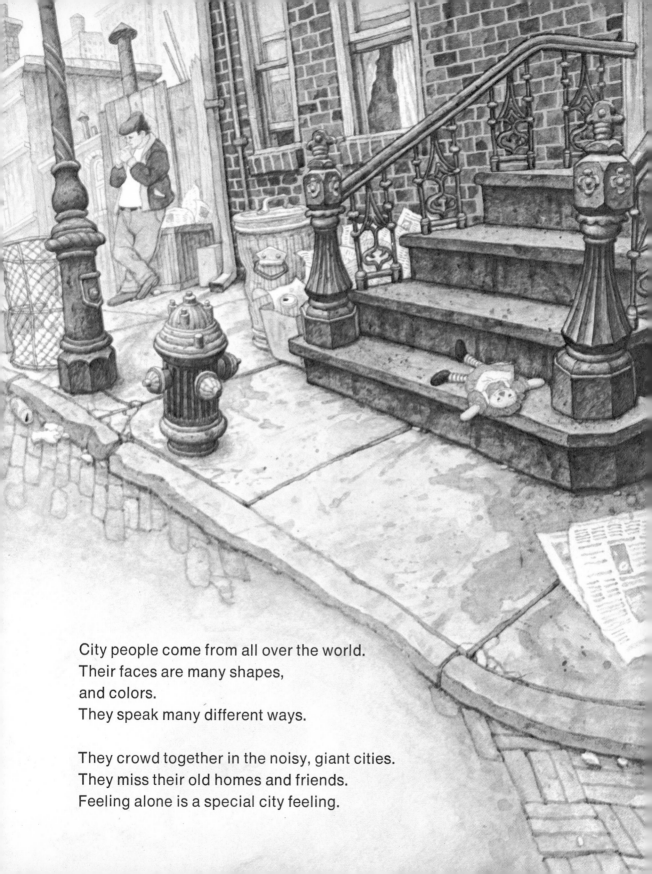

City people come from all over the world.
Their faces are many shapes,
and colors.
They speak many different ways.

They crowd together in the noisy, giant cities.
They miss their old homes and friends.
Feeling alone is a special city feeling.

Can you understand how city people feel?

Can you feel some of their feelings?

City people are sad sometimes.
But most of the time they are happy and busy.
They like the noise,
and the bright lights,
and the crowds.
They love
the beat,
beat,
beat
of the city.

Children can do many things in the city.

In the city, children find friends.
They play stickball
or hopscotch.
On hot summer streets,
they splash in the water
gushing from a fire hydrant.

People in cities love all these things.
They like the excitement.
They feel
the beat,
beat,
beat
of the city.

Can you understand how people in cities feel?

Can you feel some of their feelings?

2

Were These Cities?

Circle and Cross

You use an alphabet when you write. But people in some other parts of the world have a different way of writing. When they write, each mark stands for a whole word or even for a whole idea.

Five thousand years ago, the people who lived in Egypt made a mark like this ⊕ . It was a circle drawn around a cross. This circle-and-cross mark stood for the idea of a city. All who saw it knew that ⊕ meant a city.

How do you suppose ⊕ came to stand for the idea of a city?

Old writing of Egypt

THE CROSS

Do you know what a crosswalk is?
a crossroads? Even today, a city is a place
where many people and things and ideas
come together. In a way, a city is like
a giant crossroads.

Look carefully at the picture. Think
for a moment about what goes into a city
and what goes out of a city. People ride
trains and buses and cars into a city. They
go there to work or to shop in big stores.
They like going to a city to visit theaters
and museums and television stations.

Hartford, Connecticut

When you go to the city, do you ride on a train? Some people think this is the nicest way to go! Along the tracks, you see trains rolling into the city carrying coal in coal cars or oil in tank cars. Other trains stream out of the city, carrying refrigerators or automobiles or tennis shoes.

Some fine day, you might ride into a city in a car, on a giant highway that stretches out in front of you as smooth as a ribbon. Look at the signs on the trucks you pass. They will say BEST ORANGES, INC. or STRICTLY FRESH EGGS. A speedy little refrigerated van passes you. It says FROM COUNTRY TO YOU: FRESH CUT FLOWERS. People in cities can buy flowers picked in the country that same morning.

On the other side of the highway, trucks zoom out from the city. They carry chairs and baseball gloves and doll buggies.

When you think about a city this way, you are thinking about it as a giant crossroads. Does this crossroads idea tell you why long ago a cross ╂ became part of the city mark ⊕ ?

Testing the Crossroads Idea

You have thought about people in cars, trucks, and trains using the city as a crossroads. Here is a way to test this crossroads idea.

Airplanes follow paths or routes in the sky, from place to place. The airplanes of one large airline company fly along the paths shown on this map.

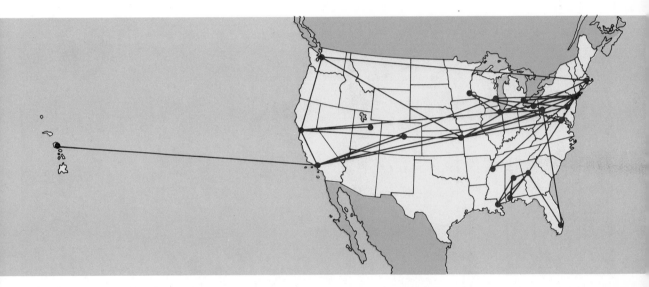

It is interesting to see how the routes make many crosses ✳ at some places. You have probably guessed that these spots ✳ , where lots of air routes cross, are cities.

Now look at a map of the United States. Use the map to find the names of the cities where the airplanes from this company land.

THE 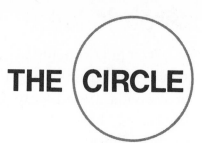CIRCLE

Look at these pictures of two old cities. What does this mark ◯ stand for?

Milan in the Middle Ages

The ◯ in the mark ⊕
stands for the wall around the city. Why
do you think people long ago built
walls around their cities?

A wall was good protection for the
people inside a city. A wall could stop
spears and arrows. A wall could stop people
with swords and people on horses.

Moscow in the Middle Ages

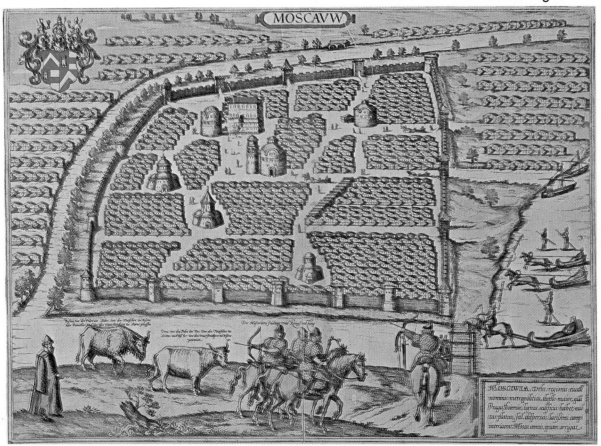

A wall cannot protect the people in a modern city from the dangers they face. People in cities today need other kinds of protection. This drawing shows some of the dangers that city people now face. And modern cities must find ways to protect their people from these dangers.

Even today, this old mark ⊕ still stands for the city. The cross ╪ stands for all the paths and routes that go into and out of a city, on land and on rivers and in the sky. The circle ◯ stands for the ways a city protects its people. You can still see a few old cities with walls around them. But most modern cities have other ways to keep their people safe.

Circleville

Along the Scioto River in Ohio, the early settlers found a very surprising sight. It looked like a great big doughnut lying on the land. The doughnut was really a dirt wall. Some of the settlers thought that the dirt wall looked like a fort.

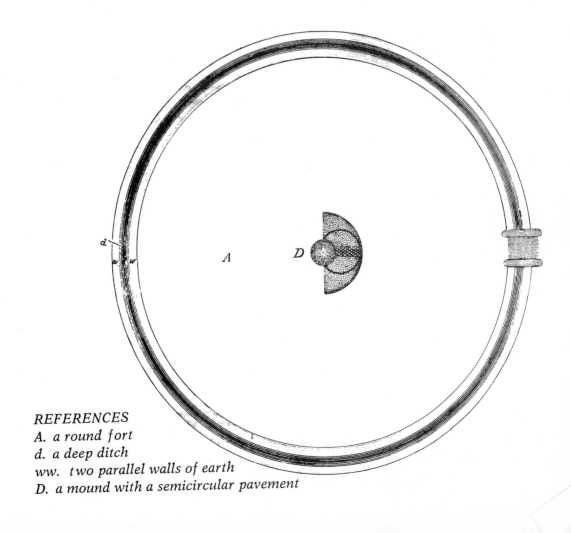

REFERENCES
A. *a round fort*
d. *a deep ditch*
ww. *two parallel walls of earth*
D. *a mound with a semicircular pavement*

The settlers had to walk more than 1,000 feet to get across from one side of the circle to the other. And the dirt wall was 20 feet high. That is higher than the room you are sitting in!

Inside and outside the wall of dirt, the ground was very clear and flat. In fact, it was just right for building a town. There were no trees to cut down and no swamps to fill in. The settlers decided that this was the place to build their town.

While the grown-ups talked and worked and drew plans for the town, the children played on the high dirt wall. They climbed its grassy sides and played hide-and-seek and raced each other rolling down the slopes.

They were sad when their parents said they were going to tear down the wall. They thought it was the best thing about their new home!

The settlers tore down the big doughnut wall. Where the circle wall once stood, the people built Circle Street. In the middle of the circle, they built a round park. In between the park and Circle Street, they made another round street called Circle Alley. Along Circle Street and Circle Alley, they built churches and schools, houses and stores, and meeting places.

Can you guess what the settlers called their town?

Naturally, they called it Circleville!

1. Court House
2. County Jail & Sheriff's Office
3. Church
4. Church
5. Church
6. District School
7. Academy
8. Red Lion Tavern
9. Canal Hotel
10. Wilkes & Wareh's Lumber Yard
11. Finley's Warehouse
12. J. & H. Smart's Provision Store
13. Circleville Bank
14. M. Bright's Tin Shop
15. Howard's Hat Store
16. Westenhover's Grocery & Bakery
17. Dr. E. B. Olds' Drug Store
18. Diffenderfer's Grocery
19. H. Sage's Jewelry Store
20. Jenkin's Grocery
21. Dr. Luckey's Office
22. Wm. McLane Cabinet Shop
23. S. Diffenderfer's House
24. Dr. E. B. Olds' House
25. James Bell's Tannery
26. Circleville Herald Office
27. F. G. Whittick's Book Bindery
28. M. Myer's Chairshop & House
29. Wilkes' Brewery
30. T. Darst's Foundry
31. Parts of Circular Ditch
32. Graveyard
33. Ohio Canal

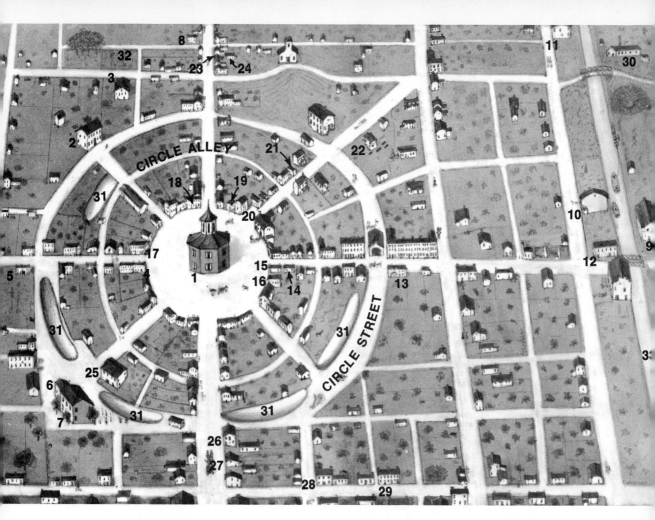

BIRD'S-EYE VIEW OF
CIRCLEVILLE, OHIO
1836
FACING SOUTH

The children missed the high grassy wall, but still it was fun to run around a town with round streets. They were proud of living in a town that was different from the back-East towns that they remembered. Those old towns were square and stiff, with the houses lined up tightly side by side.

Most of the grown-ups liked Circleville, too—at least for a while. Circleville was new and beautiful. Every house along the round streets looked special.

FOUR MAPS FOR CIRCLEVILLE

But some people missed the square corners in the towns they had left behind. They liked straight streets and rows of houses.

As the years went by, more and more people in Circleville became unhappy about their unusual town.

"It is silly to have a town with circles, when other American towns have squares," the president of the Circleville Bank declared.

"Rubbish!" snapped the gruff shopkeeper who never would let the children roll their hoops past the general store.

"We can build more houses on streets that run straight," said someone who owned land.

1837

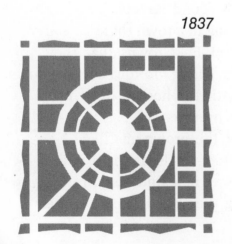

1838

Most angry of all were the people around the town circle, because pigs ran loose in the park. These people thought pigs should be kept in pens in a neat town with square corners.

Some of the townspeople formed a company, and they called it the Circleville Squaring Company. The Circleville Squaring Company bought land, moved the old houses, and made new streets.

It took almost twenty years to make Circleville a square town. By that time, children who had played hide and seek on the huge dirt wall and rolled down its grassy slopes were mothers and fathers. Many of them remembered those early days, and sometimes they were sorry things had changed. They told their children stories about the high doughnut of dirt that lay on the land. They told them about the days when Circleville had round streets.

1849

1856

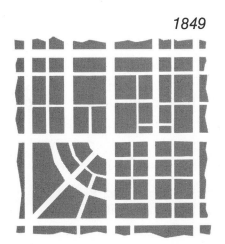

WAS THIS A CITY?

Remember the mark ⊕ for city? Could the wall at Circleville once have been the edge of an Indian city? Could the wall of dirt have protected the Indians and their children who lived there long ago? How can you tell?

How do you find out if an old, old place was once a city? What questions do you need to ask yourself? Where do you look for the answers?

One scientist, who studied many old cities, decided there were eight tests. You can use these tests to help decide whether or not a place was a city long ago. They can help you test any old, old place to see if it was once a city where people lived and children played.

1. Size Test

A city has many people living close together. More than 7,000 people must have lived in a place before it could be called a city. One test for a city is to find out if 7,000 or more people lived there.

2. Work Test

A city is a place where many of the people are specialists. A specialist does only one kind of work. Some specialists make only pots or cloth. Others build houses or add numbers or make spears. One test for a city is to find out if many people were specialists.

3. Food Test

A city has to have a supply of food for its people. Farmers had to produce more food than their families could eat. They paid some of the extra food to the city rulers. The rest they sold or traded to the people who worked at other jobs. Something extra is called a surplus. One test for a city is to find out if the farmers produced surplus food.

4. Trade Test

Cities are often built where trails cross, where rivers meet, or where ships can dock. That means that the people can travel to distant places to trade some of their corn, gold, or cloth for copper, salt, or shells. One test for a city is to find out if the people traded for goods from distant places.

34

5. Building Test

Another test for a city is to find out if there were many large buildings for the people to use.

6. Writing Test

Another test for a city is to find out if the people could write.

7. Science Test

Another test for a city is to find out if the people knew how to measure distances, add and subtract numbers, and keep track of time.

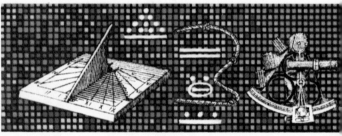

8. Government Test

The last test for a city is to find out if the people were ruled in some way.

You need evidence to know if a place passes the eight city tests. In order to know if an old, old place was once a city, you need to find evidence for the size test, work test, food test, trade test, building test, writing test, science test, and government test.

Tikal: Where Is There?

In the jungles of Guatemala is a place called Tikal. At Tikal are many old stone buildings. When scientists found Tikal, all the stone buildings were covered with vines and trees. Nobody had lived there for hundreds of years. Could Tikal once have been a city? Look at the evidence to find out.

The rocky piece of land sticking out like a thumb into the Caribbean Sea is called the Yucatan Peninsula. Near the bottom of the peninsula are the ruins of Tikal. You can get to Tikal by flying from New Orleans to Guatemala City. Just north of Guatemala City is Tikal.

AIR ROUTE TO TIKAL

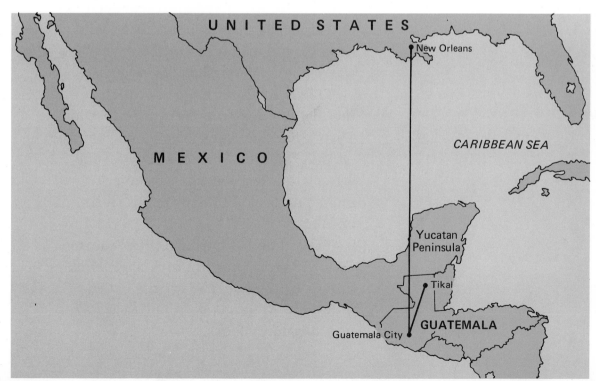

A tall rain forest covers Tikal. Spider monkeys play high up in the trees. Hawks, parrots, and hummingbirds fly through the high branches. Jaguars prowl below.

Waterholes and marshes break the forest. Here and there, the forest opens out into savannas, or grasslands. Deer, wild turkeys, and wild pigs live there, near the waterholes and marshes.

The climate is hot, especially during the dry months from February to May. Then come the rains. The rains continue off and on until October. They fill the waterholes. The waterholes are very important because there are few rivers or lakes.

The thumb that forms the Yucatan Peninsula is a very big rock shelf sticking up out of the sea. The rock is called limestone, which is soft and easy to cut into building blocks.

Today, almost two million Mayan Indians live on the Yucatan Peninsula. Most of them are farmers who grow maize. Maize is a type of corn. They also grow beans, pumpkins, and squash. Every two or three years, in early winter, the farmers have to cut down trees and bushes to clear a new patch for their cornfields. The word for cornfield is *milpa.*

In the dry season, the farmers burn the cut-down trees and bushes on their fields. The ashes are good fertilizer. Then, the farmers poke holes through the ash into the soil. They plant the maize seed. They plant bean and pumpkin and squash seeds in the *milpa,* too.

The rains come, and the plants shoot up through the ground. They grow rapidly. At harvest time, the farmers gather their crops. Everyone has food for the year.

Crops can be planted in the *milpa* only for one or two more years. Then the soil is worn out. The farmers must then find a new patch of forest to cut and burn to clear a new *milpa.* The circle of growing and harvesting food will begin all over again.

Long, long ago, before Columbus sailed to America, the Mayan people grew food in just this way. This was the place, and these were the people who long ago built Tikal.

THE TEMPLE OF THE GIANT JAGUAR

One mile from the airport, in the heart of Tikal, a great silent plaza lies in the sun. Once, long ago, it looked like the drawing below. Today, the great plaza at Tikal looks like the picture on page 39.

In the great plaza stands Temple I. It is made of great blocks of limestone, and it is shaped like a pyramid. A pyramid looks like this.

There are three small rooms and a roof comb on top of the pyramid. A roof comb is a decoration like a king's crown or the crest of a beautiful bird. Wooden beams lie over the doorways to the three small rooms. A jaguar with sharp, curving claws is carved on one of the beams. That is why Temple I is sometimes called the Temple of the Giant Jaguar.

Scientists have found out what was in Temple I by making careful tunnels through the floors and walls. Under the floor of the back room, they found one of the richest tombs in Tikal. Inside the tomb was the skeleton of a man lying on a stone bench.

Around the skeleton were pieces of bone with pictures carved on them. These pictures showed seven Mayan gods taking a canoe trip, and three *chacs*, or rain gods, catching fish.

Other carvings and pictures on jars in the tomb showed lords and prisoners.

The scientists decided that the pyramid was once a temple. Inside the pyramid is the tomb of a man who must have been important. Below the pyramid is a great plaza, where people could gather. High on top of the pyramid, priests might have called out to their gods, long, long ago. They could have called the rain god and the sun god to ask them to make the maize grow sweet and tall.

MESSAGES EVERYWHERE

Carved and painted messages are everywhere in Tikal—on limestone, on bones, and on jade—outside temples and deep inside tombs—on bowls, pots, roads, walls, and on stones set in the ground.

Messages are everywhere. But the scientists can read only a few. They have even found three books in other Mayan places. They are made of bark paper with thin pieces of wood for covers. The scientists cannot read very much in these books, either. Mostly, they can read the numbers.

Number Messages

Mayan children must have learned to count easily by using their fingers and toes. With their fingers, they could have counted by fives. With all their fingers and toes, they could have counted by twenties. Practice counting by fives and by twenties so you can learn how the Mayas counted.

COUNTING BY FIVES

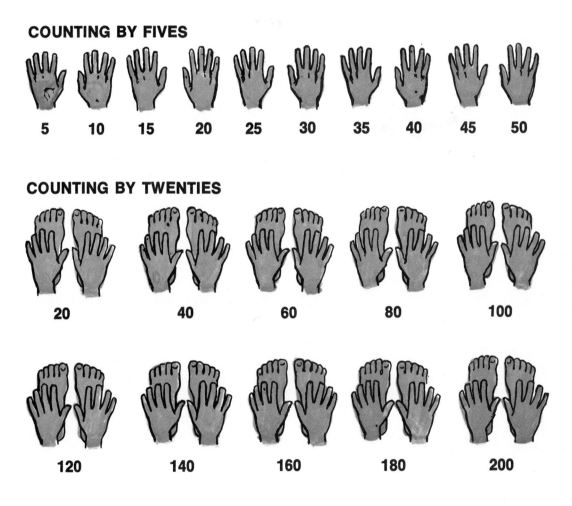

5   10   15   20   25   30   35   40   45   50

COUNTING BY TWENTIES

20   40   60   80   100

120   140   160   180   200

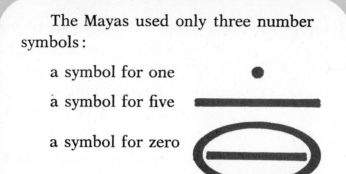

The Mayas used only three number symbols:

a symbol for one

a symbol for five

a symbol for zero

Here is how the Mayas counted to five:

one

two

three

four

five

Here is how they counted from six to ten:

six

seven

eight

nine

ten

Can you figure out how they counted to nineteen? Remember • is one and ▬ is five. Eleven looks like this:

eleven

• one of the ones

two of the fives

Mayan children learned to put their number symbols on top of each other. You could write that way, too. This is how it would look:

twenty $\begin{smallmatrix}2\\0\end{smallmatrix}$ forty $\begin{smallmatrix}4\\0\end{smallmatrix}$ sixty $\begin{smallmatrix}6\\0\end{smallmatrix}$

The Mayas wrote twenty with a dot on top of a zero, like this: ⬭. This meant one twenty and no ones. Here is how they wrote forty and sixty:

forty •• two twenties
⬭ no ones

sixty ••• three twenties
⬭ no ones

The Mayas wrote one hundred as five twenties and no ones, like this: ⬭.

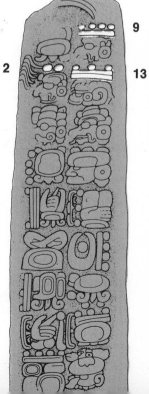

Here is a message carved on a stone. See if you can read the numbers 2, 9, and 13. Can you find the number 4? the number 17? the number 3? How many other numbers can you find?

Picture Messages

Each small square picture carved on this stone is called a glyph. A glyph is a mark that stands for an idea, the way  stands for city. Scientists know what only a few of the Mayan glyphs mean. They do know that the glyph that stood for Tikal looked like this:

Four other glyphs looked like this:

Bird Jaguar   *Capture*

Jewelled Skull   *Yaxchilan*

Using these glyphs, scientists were able to "read" how Bird Jaguar and a helper captured Jewelled Skull and another enemy at a place called Yaxchilan. Can you read this message carved in stone?

Mayan Calendars

The Mayas kept calendars, and they counted time in several different ways. One way of counting time used *kin, uinal,* and *tun*—something like our day, month, and year.

kin = 1 day
uinal = 20 days
tun = 360 days

They also had two bigger blocks of time that we do not have.

katun = 7,200 days
bactun = 144,000 days

Each block of time had its own glyph. Using these glyphs, scientists can read one great carved stone set in the ground at Tikal. It shows a count of 1 million 315 thousand and 80 days.

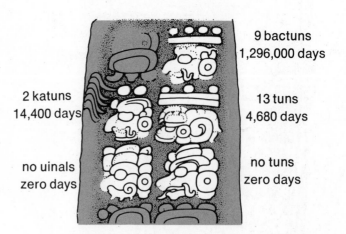

9 bactuns
1,296,000 days

2 katuns
14,400 days

13 tuns
4,680 days

no uinals
zero days

no tuns
zero days

Can you guess on what day this stone was set in the ground? This stone was placed in Tikal 1,315,080 days after the first day on the Mayan calendar.

GROWING UP IN TIKAL

Beautiful Children

Mayan mothers and fathers loved their children. They wanted their boys and girls to be good and beautiful in the Mayan way.

When a Mayan baby was born, its parents put the child's head between two boards in a special cradle. The baby stayed in the cradle for many days. This made the front of its head flat. The baby's flat head made its nose seem long and beautiful, like the nose of the giant jaguar.

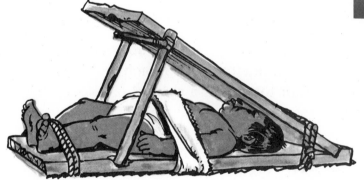

Next, a little ball was hung in front of the baby's forehead. The ball rested between the child's eyes, right at the top of the nose. The baby would stare at the ball until both eyes pointed in. Crossed eyes were beautiful to the Mayan people.

Every mother and father carefully followed the Mayan rules to take good care of their babies. They wanted their children to be good Mayas. Each mother and father wanted their children to be beautiful in the Mayan way.

Mayan boys and girls were given four names. A boy might have a name like this:

Ah Kukum "the feather," his given name
Chan the name of his father's family
Chel the name of his mother's family
Cuy "the owl," his nickname

A Mayan Day

Early in the morning, the women got up to start the fires. Three stones held each fire. So the number three was a symbol for the work of women.

In the early dawn, the men left to work in the *milpas.* Each *milpa* had four corners. So the number four was a symbol for the work of men.

Everybody drank good maize-flavored water for breakfast. Wives made soft maize balls with hot peppers and wrapped them in leaves for the husbands and sons to take to the fields.

On the way to his *milpa,* a father would look at his deer traps. He would teach his sons how to set the trap and how to say the hunting prayer: "I have need."

In the *milpa,* the father and his sons would pull up weeds. Sometimes they stopped to gather honey from their beehives or to harvest beans and pumpkins and squash. Sometimes the young boys grew tired of work and sneaked off to hunt cacao beans to make chocolate.

At home, mothers taught their daughters to spin the wild cotton and to grind maize for *tortillas.* The family would eat these flat corncakes with their supper of deer stew and hot peppers.

The men returned from the fields in the early afternoon. Tikal even had a building where they could go for steam baths.

In the evening, while the grown-ups talked, the children played. Then they went to sleep on mats, with cotton blankets for covers.

Mayan Ceremonies

When Mayan boys were fourteen years old and Mayan girls were twelve, they were considered grown-up. A priest, or *chilan,* held the coming-of-age ceremony for several of them at once. An important man was always chosen to be the *chilan.* Four old men were chosen to act as *chacs,* the rain gods. On the special day, parents, friends, and children came to the temple or to the courtyard of the *chilan's* house. A clean square of ground was spread with fresh leaves. The *chacs* sat at the four corners, holding a cord that went around the square. The children were placed inside the cord.

The *chilan* lighted a fire so the smoke would purify the children. The *chacs* placed a white cloth on the head of each child. One by one, all the children told their sins. The *chilan* tapped every child nine times on the forehead. He sprinkled each with water and took off the white cloth.

Each mother then cut a string around her daughter's waist that held a red seashell. For only little girls wore the shell. Each father cut the white bead that his son wore stuck to the hair on the top of his head. For only little boys wore the bead. Now the Mayan girls were women. Now the Mayan boys were men.

When a man and woman were married, everybody gathered at the house of the bride's parents. The *chilan* lighted a fire so the smoke would make the house pure. He blessed the bride and groom. Everyone sat down to eat. That is what a wedding was like in Tikal.

The bride and groom built their house close to the house of the bride's parents. First, they laid stones to make a good floor. Then they put up four posts to hold up the four corners of the house. They made the walls from thin strips of wood covered with *adobe*. *Adobe* is dried mud. They made the roof with poles. Over the poles, they set tightly thatched palm leaves to keep out the rain. They whitened the walls of the house with lime.

When Mayans died, they were buried beneath the floors of their homes. Their families put maize in their mouths so that they would have something to eat in the other life. The people of Tikal wanted their loved ones to be comfortable, even after they were no longer living on this earth.

WHEN TIME STOPPED

All over the Mayan lands, great stones were carved for the rulers and set in the ground. These great carved stones are called stelae. Dates were carved on the stelae to show when new rulers took the throne.

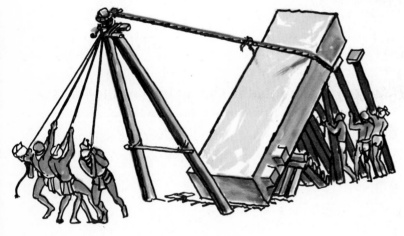

At Tikal there are more than 200 carved stones and altars. For many hundreds of years, the Mayans added a carving for each new ruler.

Then something very mysterious happened. All the carving stopped in Tikal and in the Mayan lands nearby. No more dates were carved. People stopped setting the stone markers in the ground. No more temples were built. Time seemed to stop. What happened?

Remember how Tikal parents used boards to flatten their babies' heads? Remember how the flat heads made the children's noses long and beautiful, like the beautiful nose of the jaguar?

In Tikal and other Mayan places, many of the noses on statues are broken and smashed. Could the people have killed their rulers? Could they have smashed all the carvings on the temples?

A missionary named Father Avendano came to the Mayan lands long after Columbus had come to America. Once he was lost in the jungles near Tikal. He found silent ruins. All the rulers and all the people had gone from Tikal. There were no more babies with beautiful noses like the jaguar's.

Father Avendano found many old buildings in the jungles. He called them "apartments." All were empty.

"Although they were very high and my strength was little, I climbed up them," he wrote in his diary.

How sad and empty and mysterious it must have seemed to him as he looked out from the high pyramids.

People are still puzzled by the mysteries of Tikal.

If the people killed the rulers and broke the stelae, why did they leave afterward? What did happen to the rulers? What did happen to the people?

No one knows for sure. No one knows why the people left Tikal. All anyone knows for sure is that suddenly life at Tikal came to an end.

Zimbabwe: Where Is There?

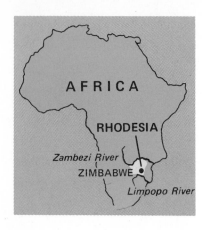

Look at the map of Africa and find the country of Rhodesia. There, north of the Limpopo River and south of the Zambezi River, is a place called Zimbabwe.

"Zimbabwe" is an old, old African word. Some scientists think it means "houses of stone." Others think it means "great house." Nobody knows for sure.

There are other puzzles about Zimbabwe. Nobody lives in Zimbabwe now, among the empty stone ruins. But people did live there long ago. Who were these people? Who built Zimbabwe? Why did they build it? Was Zimbabwe once a city?

GRASS AND ROCKS

The hills between the Limpopo and the Zambezi rivers are low and rolling. From May to September, the land is dry and hot. Here and there, low bushy trees shade the ground. Then the rainy season starts. After the rains, a short tough grass grows. The land, with the grass and trees, looks like a park. The land is a savanna.

Long ago on the savanna, herds of zebras and antelope lived on the grass. Meat-eaters like lions and leopards killed the grass-eaters for food. People hunted all these animals. Some people tamed grass-eating cattle and kept them safe in herds. That was the way of the savanna for many years.

Here and there across the savanna, big chunks of hard rock stick up from the land. This hard rock is granite. The granite was there long before people came to Zimbabwe. And it is still there today.

RUINS OF STONE

The mysterious stone ruins of Zimbabwe stand on the savanna, near a group of granite rocks. In a little valley, great stone walls, thirty feet high and fourteen feet thick, form a big circle. The circle of ruins is called the Temple.

Inside the Temple are smaller walls. Many of them have crumbled. Still standing is one tall tower. This tall tower is a puzzle inside the puzzle of the Temple. It is solid rock. No treasure is buried in it. No graves are there. No one knows why the tower was built. No one knows what it was used for.

Not far from the Temple, a rocky hill sticks up out of the valley. Between the granite boulders on the hill are many broken stone walls. The big rocks and the thick walls look like a fortress high above the valley. Zimbabwe hill, with its ruins, is called the Acropolis.

These are the pieces to an old, old puzzle on the savanna of Rhodesia. The Temple is one piece of the puzzle. The Acropolis is another piece of the puzzle. Maybe, if you fit all the pieces together, you can solve the puzzle of Zimbabwe.

THE STORY OF THE WALLS

The finest walls at Zimbabwe are in the Temple. Look closely at them. What do you notice?

Not all the walls of Zimbabwe are the same. There are three kinds of walls. They tell a story. See if you can find the story in the walls. How is each wall different? Which wall is the oldest? Which wall is the newest?

WALL 1

WALL 2

Scientists think that WALL 1 is the oldest. The stones are set on the ground. They zigzag and do not fit together tightly. Scientists have also found very old pots in the earth near WALL 1.

WALL 2 is set in a flat trench in the ground. The stones run straight, and they fit well together. Newer pots have been found in the earth near WALL 2.

WALL 3 is the newest and the poorest wall at Zimbabwe. Scientists believe that the people who built WALL 2 were driven from Zimbabwe. Their secret of building fine walls was lost. Those who returned could only build poor walls, like WALL 3.

WALL 3

Here is how scientists think that the best walls were made.

First, the people of Zimbabwe made huge fires to heat the solid granite that stuck up from the land. Next, they threw cold water on the hot rock to make it crack. They used iron points to trim the granite into blocks. Other workers pulled the heavy blocks on wooden sleds into place. Finally, trenches were dug, and builders balanced the stone blocks, one on top of another, to make the walls. They balanced the blocks so well that they did not need cement to hold them together.

About 300 workers were probably needed to build the Temple walls. About 15,000 tons of stone were used. The walls of Zimbabwe are among the most famous ruins in southern Africa.

THE STORY OF THE PEOPLE

The people who built the fine walls, like WALL 2, were probably the Rozwi. Scientists think that the Rozwi came to Zimbabwe from another part of Africa.

In those days, the savanna between the two rivers was ruled by a powerful African king. The king was called the Monomatapa. The people served their ruler well. They built fine walls. They fought his enemies.

Finally, the Rozwi conquered the Monomatapa. The Rozwi Mambo, or chief of the Rozwi, became king of the savanna. He ruled all the tribes on the land between the two rivers.

The Rozwi built a palace for the Mambo at Zimbabwe. Around the palace they put up the stone walls now called the Temple. They also built the tall stone tower.

The Mambo lived in the palace with his court. They all dressed in cotton robes. Threads of thin gold wire were woven into the cotton robes.

The Rozwi believed that their Mambo was perfect. Few people were allowed to see him. The Mambo used a secret path to go to the round tower. He used a secret trail up to the Acropolis. When people came to speak to him, the Mambo sat behind a curtain.

The Rozwi called their Mambo the Lion. When the Mambo died, they said his spirit lived on in the body of a lion. When he died, all the village fires were put out. The people started new fires from the royal fire of the new Mambo. This is how the Rozwi showed that they would obey their new ruler.

Gold from Rozwi mines was traded far and wide. Cloth and dishes were brought from China, glass beads from India and Europe. All these and more have been found in the earth behind the walls of Zimbabwe.

The end came when Ngoni warriors killed the last Mambo. They burned everything at Zimbabwe. They carried off the cattle, the women, and the children.

Only a few Rozwi ever returned to Zimbabwe. They tried to build walls again. They tried to keep the old ways. But after a while, they too went away. The walls of Zimbabwe were left empty.

THE STORY OF ZIMBABWE HILL

Many years after the Rozwi left, visitors began coming to Zimbabwe. The walls were empty. The Africans who lived nearby saluted the hill at Zimbabwe. It was a sacred place. But no one knew why.

The visitors told stories about the rock houses of Zimbabwe. But they said that people from lands across the seas had built them. They did not know that Zimbabwe hill was a sacred place where the Rozwi kings were buried.

Seven bird-figures were found on Zimbabwe hill. The Zimbabwe birds stood on round red mounds in a room made of huge granite rocks and walls. One by one the birds were taken away. The people who took them did not know who had made them or what they were for.

The Zimbabwe birds are now in a museum. Scientists think they were used to ask the god Mwari to send rain to the savanna. The Rozwi believed that living people could not speak to Mwari. Only the dead kings could carry messages to him. So the Rozwi made bird-figures, each one for a dead Rozwi king who could speak to Mwari. The figures stood in the sacred room on Zimbabwe hill, where the priests said prayers. The seven bird-figures made scientists wonder if Zimbabwe hill was like a church to the Rozwi.

Another discovery also made scientists wonder if Zimbabwe hill was a sacred place. Messages can be sent in a surprising way from the hill to the valley. There is a cave on Zimbabwe hill, near the place where the bird-figures were found. When someone speaks in a natural voice in the cave, the words can be heard far away, in one spot in the valley. That one spot is the Temple. Nowhere else in the valley can the voice from the cave be heard.

Did the people of Zimbabwe know this? Did they build the Temple so the priests could talk to the Mambo? Did only the Mambo know of the secret cave? No one knows for sure. This is just one more piece to fit into the puzzle of Zimbabwe.

Mohenjo-daro: Where Is There?

North of India is a long wall of rocky, snowy peaks. This great wall of mountains is called the Himalayas.

The Himalaya range is nearly 1,500 miles long. The peaks of this mountain range are very very high. Mount Everest is one of the peaks in the Himalayas. It is the highest mountain in the world.

Way up in the northern Himalayas, a river begins. It is called the Indus. Fed by melting mountain snows, the Indus River rises and tumbles down a deep gorge.

The river flows west around the end of the great wall of peaks and south onto a hot, dry plain in Pakistan. There, four smaller rivers flow into the great river. They are the tributaries of the Indus. From the plain, the Indus flows over low land and out to the Arabian Sea.

Along the Indus River in Pakistan is a very old place called Mohenjo-daro. Here, scientists have found many brick buildings. Most of them are broken down. Some are almost covered over with river mud.

On a low hill near the river is a high platform made of bricks.

Scientists think that once, long ago, a great shed stood on top of the brick platform. The people of Mohenjo-daro may have stored grain in the shed. The grain shed must have looked like this.

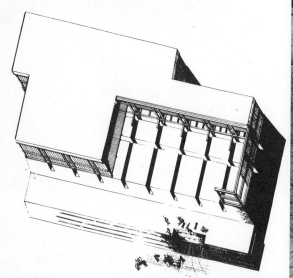

All around the grain shed are crisscrossing streets and the ruins of brick buildings. If you walked in a circle around this place, you would walk for three miles.

No one has lived in Mohenjo-daro for more than three thousand years. Long before the Mayas built Tikal and the Rozwi conquered Zimbabwe, the people of Mohenjo-daro built the grain shed and the brick buildings and the streets. But was this old place called Mohenjo-daro a city?

TREASURES IN THE MUD

North of Mohenjo-daro, in the snowy peaks of the Himalayas, the Indus and its four tributaries begin their tumbling journey. Each spring, the snow melts and makes the rivers grow big. They plunge down from the high mountains, carrying rocks, gravel, and dirt. The rocks and gravel do not go far—they are heavy and sink. But the waters of the five rivers carry the dirt down from the mountains and out onto the plain below.

One by one, the tributaries join the Indus. The river becomes bigger and bigger. Soon it spills over its banks. The muddy water spreads over the flat land around Mohenjo-daro. The old soil is made rich by the new layer of river mud.

Today farmers in Pakistan plant crops along the Indus River banks. The people of Mohenjo-daro planted crops there more than three thousand years ago.

Each spring, the Indus flooded the plain and left its river mud behind. Each spring, farmers planted seeds in the muddy soil. The seeds sprouted and grew. The summer heat spread over the land, and the plants ripened quickly. Then the harvest came.

After the harvest, the farmers rested. The next spring, when the rivers grew fat again from the melting snow, the farmers knew it was time to plant once more.

The people of Mohenjo-daro built dams to keep the Indus River where it belonged. But some years the mountain snows were extra deep. When the snows melted, the rivers grew extra big. The flood waters poured over the dams, filling houses with water and mud.

Some houses were ruined, or even washed away. Everything was buried in the mud. The people lost their fish hooks. They lost their pots and their copper axes.

When the flood waters went down, the people built new houses on top of their old ones. They made new fish hooks and pots and copper axes. When the next flood came, some people lost their houses and their tools again. Once more, they built new houses and made new tools.

Several times all the streets and the houses of Mohenjo-daro were buried under river mud. In the layers of mud and bricks are the fish hooks, pots, and copper axes that the people lost long, long ago. Scientists have uncovered many of these. They have found razors. They have found saws with small pieces of cotton cloth stuck to them.

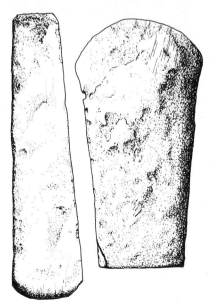

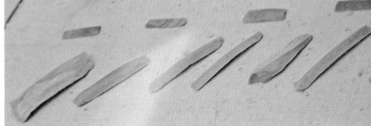

The evidence at Mohenjo-daro is buried deep in the mud and bricks of many river floods. Piece by piece, like buried treasures, scientists have uncovered the evidence. That is how they know about the people of Mohenjo-daro and the way they lived.

LIFE IN MOHENJO-DARO

People and Things

It is hard to know what people were like long ago. But scientists who dug into the mud at Mohenjo-daro found a few statues of people. One stone statue shows a man with a beard. He wears a robe, and his hair is tied back with a band. His eyes are almost closed. The scientists think that he was a priest or a king.

Other statues are clay models of women. Each one wears many necklaces. On their heads are large decorations. These women may have been mother goddesses.

Some of the people wore fine jewelry. Many pieces have been found buried in the mud. Beads, rings, and bracelets were made of turquoise from Iran and gold from India. Copper from Afghanistan was made into bowls and dishes.

MOHENJO-DARO IMPORTS

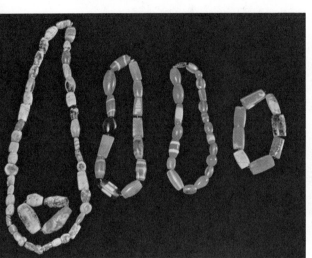

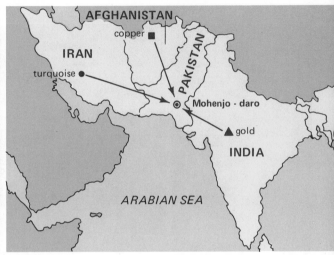

The children of Mohenjo-daro played with toys. The scientists dug up small toy oxcarts, with wheels that turn. They found whistles, too, and models of oxen with heads that move.

The people of Mohenjo-daro knew how to write. On their pots and seals they made picture signs. Scientists have found more than three hundred of these signs. But they cannot read any of them. If they could, they might learn a lot more about life in Mohenjo-daro long ago.

The people also knew how to weigh and measure. Scientists uncovered stone weights and pieces of balance scales. They have found measuring rods, too. One measurement is called a cubit. A cubit is the length from a person's elbow to the tip of the middle finger. It is about 20 inches long.

Buildings and Streets

The houses of Mohenjo-daro were one or two stories high and built of bricks. Each house had a courtyard. There were rooms for servants, too. Some of the houses even had bathrooms. The picture shows what the houses must have looked like.

Scientists have counted the number of house ruins at Mohenjo-daro. They think that almost twenty thousand people lived there at one time.

The main streets were about 18 cubits wide. Scientists made a map of the streets and buildings of Mohenjo-daro. They mapped the five main streets and the twelve blocks of buildings. They gave the blocks code names, like Hr and Dk, because they did not know what the people of Mohenjo-daro named their streets.

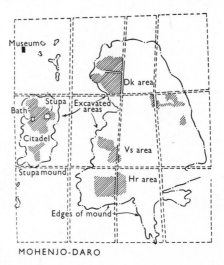

MOHENJO-DARO

The scientists also mapped the narrow lanes that ran between the houses. The map shows the houses, streets, and lanes in the Hr block of Mohenjo-daro.

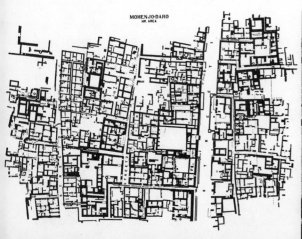

Each street had a covered drain to carry sewer water to stone pits.

A large building on one street had a room with holes in the floor. Jars were set in the holes in the floor. The building may have been a restaurant, or a place to dye cloth.

On another street was the grain shed— the largest building in Mohenjo-daro. Nearby was a large bathhouse. The main bathing tank was 23 cubits long and 14 cubits wide. All around it were small rooms. People must have come to the bathhouse to take warm baths and to talk with their friends.

HOW DID IT END?

No one knows for sure how Mohenjo-daro came to an end. No one has lived there for three thousand years. For many years, visitors saw only a wide desert where there was no life.

Then the scientists discovered Mohenjo-daro. They uncovered evidence in the mud. They found skeletons in the streets and in the houses. Skeletons were in the streets at the highest levels. Skeletons were in the latest houses. There were sword cuts on the skeletons. Mohenjo-daro must have been attacked in its last days.

No one really knows who attacked Mohenjo-daro. But when the end came, the people were weak. More and more floods had come. The houses had to be built again and again. Wood was hard to find. More and more floods came. There were many people to feed. Crops were hard to grow. After every flood, the people had to work harder and harder.

When the attack came, the people were weak and tired. The end came swiftly. Mohenjo-daro was no more.

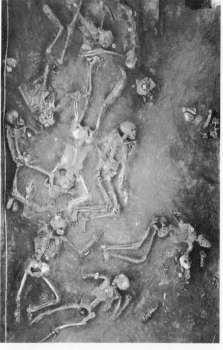

3

Where on Earth?

A Caravan in Cairo

Questions fly down the streets of the city. Shouts are heard at every door. A caravan comes to Cairo!

Look there! Four long lines of camels come from the desert. Count them. Eighty camels carry bags of gold. How much do the bags weigh? Three hundred pounds each. What riches!

Look, the slaves. Five hundred of
them. Each one carries a bar of gold.

Watch out! Soldiers come this way.
Dust and sand choke the air.

Who is it? Who comes?

Mansa Musa? Who is he?

In the great caravan to Cairo came camel drivers, soldiers, and slaves. Doctors, merchants, teachers, and servants came too. The royal family and the court rode on the backs of camels across the desert. It has been said that sixty thousand people were counted in the caravan of Mansa Musa, ruler of the Mandingo people, King of the Gold Mines.

Where does he come from? How far has he traveled?

The empire of Mali? Where is that?

It has been said that the empire of Mali was four months of travel long and four months wide. It was a land to the west, across the desert. It was west of the Ahaggar Mountains.

An old map of Mali shows Mansa Musa with a piece of gold.

Mansa Musa ruled over all the lands at the edge of the Niger River. He ruled the gold mines of Wangara, and the copper mines of Takedda. He ruled the salt mines of Taghaza. Niani, Jenne, Gao, and Timbuktu were his cities.

In the cities of Mali, mosques were built. For Islam was the religion of the Mandingo people. Their king, Mansa Musa, was on his way to the holy city of Mecca. The time had come for the *hajj*—the journey to Mecca. The king would be one who has been to the holy city. He would be a *haji.* That was why his caravan was in Cairo.

The mosque in the city of Mecca

STEPPE AND DESERT

In the year 1492, Columbus crossed the Atlantic Ocean. More than 150 years earlier, Mansa Musa crossed an ocean of desert. That was in 1324, the year of Mansa Musa's *hajj*.

MANSA MUSA'S *HAJJ*

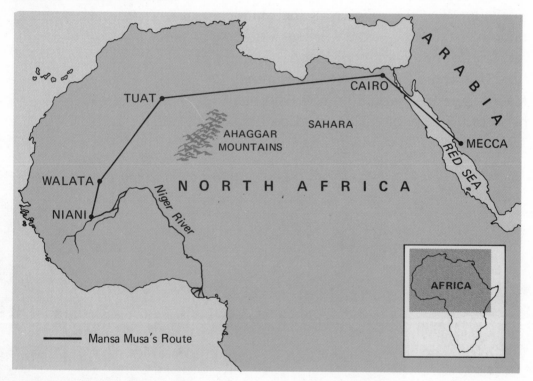

Mansa Musa's Route

North from Niani to Walata went the king's caravan. North over the dry plain called the steppe. Almost no trees grow on the steppe, and only short grass. Little rain falls on this land at the edge of the desert.

North from Walata to Tuat, the great caravan moved, day and night, under the hot sun and the cold stars of the Sahara sky. Desert air is dry and clear. The hard ground and the sand reflect the hot sun during the day. After the sun goes down, the earth gives up its heat quickly. Strong winds blow. The nights are bitter cold.

Many years, no rain at all falls on the desert. When the rain does come, it comes in a swift, short storm. But the ground is hard and dry. It grows few plants to hold back the water. Floods rush down the dry stream beds called *wadis*. The rain storm moves on, and the *wadis* dry up again. The rain water slowly seeps underground toward an oasis. The ground is hard and dry once more.

HOW AN OASIS GETS ITS WATER

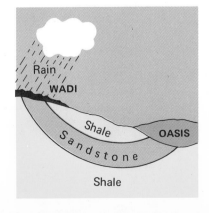

At a large oasis, where the water is good even in dry years, date palms grow. People of the desert say that the date palm has its feet in water and its head in fire. Its roots can find water, but its high branches bake in the sun. At large oases, where date palms grow, people build houses of sun-dried brick or mud.

Most of the oases are far apart and small. Some are so small they can be hidden by bandits. The bandits wait to destroy the caravans that look for water. But Mansa Musa's soldiers protected him from bandits. His guides knew how to find each oasis by following the sun, the stars, and the wind patterns on the sand.

East from Tuat toward Cairo went Mansa Musa's caravan. Across the desert moved the camels on wide, padded feet. Their hoodlike eyelids kept out the blowing sand. Fat stored in their humps kept them going many miles a day. They did not even have to stop for water.

In the middle of the Sahara, Mansa Musa might have seen the rock pictures of Tassili-n-Ajjer. Giraffe, elephant, monkey, and lion pictures are carved in the rock. These rock pictures show that long ago the desert was different. Many thousands of years before Mansa Musa's *hajj*, rain fell there. Grass and trees grew on the plains and plateaus of North Africa. In those days, the Sahara was a land of plenty.

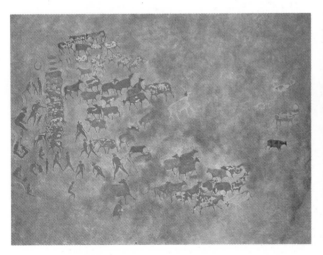

Onward moved the king. Soon his caravan would be near Cairo. After Cairo, he would be near his goal. He would be near Mecca, the place where Mohammed, the prophet of Islam, was born.

TIMBUKTU

Mansa Musa reached his goal. And when he returned to Mali, he brought back many ideas and plans from his *hajj*. Poets, architects, and scholars also returned with him. His cities grew in importance.

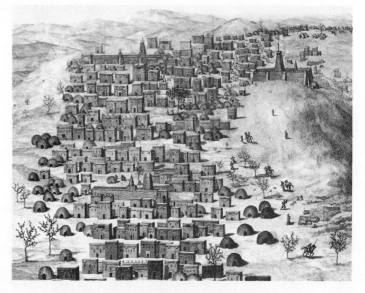

Timbuktu became a great city of learning. Mansa Musa once invited a famous scholar from another land to teach at the university there. When the scholar came to the university, he talked with the other scholars. Then he turned right around and left Timbuktu. He said that his learning was not great enough. He did not return for many years. He studied and he studied until he thought he knew enough to teach at the university in Timbuktu.

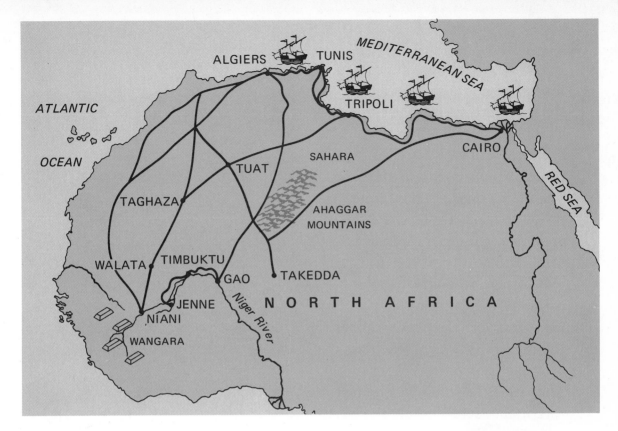

TRADE ROUTES AROUND TIMBUKTU

 Ships from Europe   Gold

AFRICA

In those days, Timbuktu was a center of trade, too. South from Cairo, Tripoli, Tunis, and Algiers came the caravans of the Arab traders bringing goods from Europe. South from Taghaza and other desert places came long lines of camels carrying salt for trade. North from Timbuktu went the camel caravans carrying the gold, ivory, spices, and animal hides brought up the Niger River by canoe. This was the rich caravan trade in the Mali city of Timbuktu.

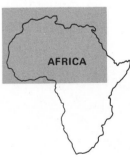

Many years later, ships from Europe began to sail along the coast of Africa. On rivers in boats, and over land on the backs of donkeys, Africans brought their goods to the sea. The places on the sea became the new trade centers. Fewer and fewer caravans came to Timbuktu.

In time, the city became weak. It was captured by invaders, and the teachers left the university. Very little news or trade crossed the desert. The city of learning was almost forgotten. Here and there, men remembered just one thing —the gold of Timbuktu.

Cities on the Land

Timbuktu was built near the banks of the Niger River in Africa. Goods from Europe came by camel from coast cities of North Africa. Salt came by camel from the desert to the north. Gold, ivory, spices, and animal hides came by canoe from places along the river to the south. The city of Timbuktu stood where the camels from the desert met the canoes on the river.

CITY SITES

Are you in school now? The place where your school is built is called a school site. The place where you buy food, go to the movies, or see a doctor is called a business site. A site is a place on the land.

The site of Timbuktu was near the banks of the Niger River at the edge of the Sahara. The place where a city is built is called a city site.

Where Are Cities Built?

Are cities built on top of mountains?

Are cities built in deep canyons?

Are cities built in thick forests?

Geographers study the land. They study the cities on the land, too. Geographers don't think cities are accidents. They look for the reason a city is built where it is. They study the site of a city. And they study what the site of a city means to the people who live there.

London Bridge is falling down,

Falling down, falling down,

London Bridge is falling down,

My fair lady.

LONDON

The London Bridge song tells about a city site long ago. The city of London was first built by a bridge. It was built close to old London Bridge.

London Bridge was built across the Thames River. It was built where the tide from the sea comes up the deep river. Ships from the sea sailed up the river to the bridge. Wagons from the farms and mills crossed the river at the bridge. Wagons and ships met at London Bridge on the edge of the river near the sea.

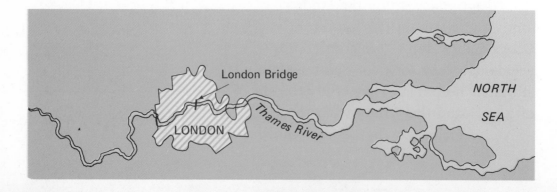

London Bridge

LONDON

Thames River

NORTH SEA

Penny and Half-Penny

Farmers came to London Bridge with wool, butter, and pigs to sell. Merchants came to London Bridge with cloth, wine, and leather to sell. They paid tolls so they could trade at the docks near London Bridge.

Here are some of the tolls farmers and merchants paid in London long ago:

A small ship pays a half-penny as toll; a large ship with sails pays one penny.

A merchant who comes to old London Bridge with a boatload of fish pays a half-penny as toll.

A farmer with a basket of hens pays one hen as toll; from a basket of eggs, he pays five eggs.

A woman who sells butter and cheese pays two pennies at Christmas time.

Rivers, Oceans, and Land

London was built at the edge of a river. Many other cities were built at the edges of rivers. Some cities were built at the edges of oceans. Some cities were built where rivers and oceans meet. Some other cities were built at the edges of mountains and plains. The edges of rivers, oceans, mountains, and plains are good city sites.

RIVER'S EDGE

Rivers are easy to cross if you can swim well and if you do not have anything to carry. But rivers are hard to cross if you can't swim or if you want to keep your corn or your wool dry.

If you want to keep your corn or your wool dry, you can cross a river best at a ford, a ferry, or a bridge. Fords, ferries, and bridges are good crossing places. They are good city sites.

A map of Paris in the Middle Ages

At fords, ferries, and bridges, roads come together. Travelers on the roads need supplies and places to sleep. Sometimes they need to sell corn or wool or to buy cotton, salt, books, or pans. Sometimes they need to see a doctor or a dressmaker. That is why cities were built where roads met at river fords, ferries, and bridges.

Paris and many other famous cities began as crossing places at rivers.

Other cities were built at the edges of rivers where deep water comes close to the land. These places were good sites for cities. The cities were ports. Ships could dock and unload cargo. Traders could buy and sell the cargo. That is why port cities were built where deep river water comes close to the land and ships can dock.

Places near river falls and rapids were good city sites. Waterwheels were built at the falls and rapids. The water power turned the millstones that ground flour, or the saws that cut logs. When people traveled along the rivers, they had to stop to unload their boats and carry them around the falls and rapids. That is why people came together and built cities near falls and rapids.

OCEAN'S EDGE

Cities were built on the edges of oceans. They were built where the water is deep and ships can dock. Many cities on the ocean's edge became great ports. Roads crossed the land and came together at the ocean ports. They met the ships that sailed the seas.

Goods were bought and sold right on the docks. And ships were built there. Wheat came by land and water into port, was put into sacks and shipped out again by land and sea. Wood came into port and was made into furniture. And the furniture was shipped out. Iron was brought into port. It was made into steel, and the steel was shipped out. Leather came into port. It was made into shoes, and the shoes were shipped out over land and sea.

Many cities were built on the edges of oceans. Seattle, Charleston, and Mobile are port cities on the edges of oceans.

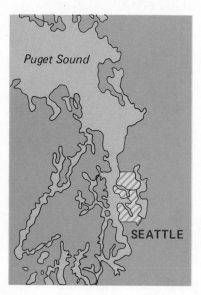

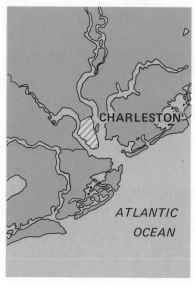

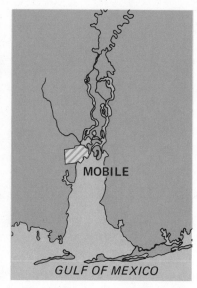

Some port cities are built on peninsulas that stick out into the ocean. Boston and San Francisco are port cities on peninsulas.

Some port cities are on estuaries at the edge of oceans. An estuary is a site where the ocean tide comes up the mouth of a large, deep river—like the site of London. Ocean ships can often sail into an estuary and dock there. Baltimore and Philadelphia are port cities on estuaries.

LAND'S EDGE

Deserts and prairies often make people think of oceans. Wind ripples the desert sand and prairie grass until they look like ocean waves. Camels that cross the desert are sometimes called "ships of the desert."

In olden times, people crossed the wide American prairie to go West. They called their covered wagons "prairie schooners." Schooners with their big sails crossed oceans of water. Prairie schooners crossed oceans of grass.

When travelers crossed a desert or a prairie, they were glad to reach the other side—just as sailors are glad to reach land. The edges of prairies or deserts, where the trails of travelers met, made good city sites. Kansas City, Omaha, Chicago, and Cincinnati were all built on the edges of prairies. They were on water edges, too. These places were good city sites for more than one reason.

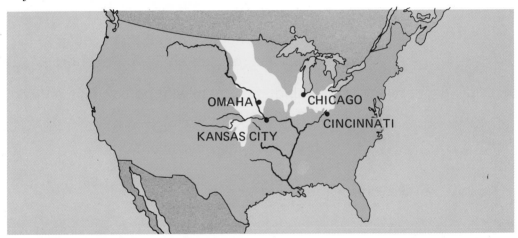

At the edges of mountains, more trails came together. Cities were built there, too. Denver and Salt Lake City are cities at the edges of mountains.

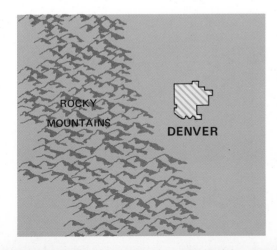

Denver

COLORADO
DENVER

Council Bluffs Rocky Mountains

Denver   Pikes Peak

GOLD RUSH

Did you hear that? Gold! Out West!

Hitch up the wagon. Let's go!

"Pike's Peak or Bust!"

In Council Bluffs, Iowa, a busy man hurried up and down the streets. All over town he ran, picking up empty sacks.

"What you doing with all them sacks?" asked a calm man sitting on his porch.

"Going to fill them with gold at Pike's Peak," said the busy man.

"Ha!" said the calm man.

"Oh yes I will," the busy man said, "even if I have to stay until fall."

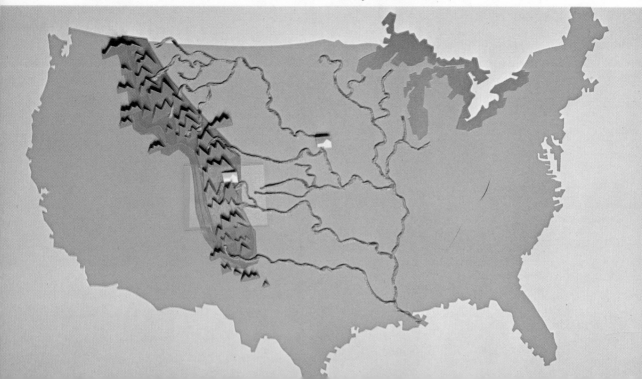

"Pike's Peak or Bust!"

Everybody was going to get rich fast. The rush for gold was on.

Over the prairie rolled the wagons. Up from the banks of the Missouri River. Up from the Kansas River. Up from the Red River and the Arkansas. Up from the great Mississippi. Over the prairie they rolled. Heading for the far-off mountains, they rolled on and on.

The green trees and soft tall grass lay farther and farther behind the gold hunters. Ahead, the prairie wind blew dry. The soil didn't look good for farming. Still, they came in wagons, looking for gold. On their wagons they painted signs.

Some miners stopped at Pike's Peak, in Colorado. Others went on, deep into the Rocky Mountains. North and south along the mountains they went, looking for gold. Sooner or later, they all came to Cherry Creek on the South Platte River. Most of the trails in and out or up and down the wall of mountains met at Cherry Creek. People began to gather there, to talk, to rest, to buy food and supplies. A city started to grow at Cherry Creek—a city called Denver.

"Go-Backs"

Gold was there in the mountains. But it was hard to get out of the rocks. Some people had machinery to mine the gold. But most people did not. And soon they ran out of supplies and money. They gave up.

Someone wrote down what a "Go-Back" needed to return home broke:

1 ragged coat
1 pair pants, hanging together by shreds
1 old black hat
1½ shoes, looking like fried bacon
00,000 ounces of gold

Down from the mountains the gold hunters came. Back out onto the prairie they walked or rode. Down to the rivers they went, to homes east of the Mississippi. This time they painted different signs on their wagons.

AFTER THE GOLD RUSH

Near Pike's Peak, where the trails met on the South Platte River at Cherry Creek, the town of Denver kept growing. When the gold boom started, Denver was born. When the gold boom busted, many people said that Denver would die. But it did not.

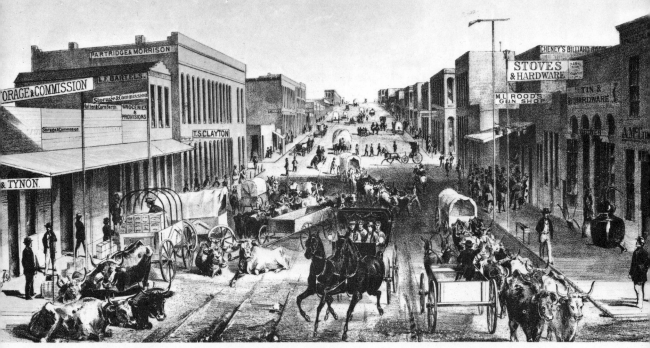

Today Denver is a big city, and still growing. It has many office buildings. Sugar beets and winter wheat are shipped to Denver. Cattle and sheep are shipped there. Miners work in the Rocky Mountain mines.

Today Denver is a big city, and still growing. How did it happen?

Roads, Railroads, Air Routes

Many miners stayed out West after the gold rush, doing what they could. Some farmed along the rivers. Some raised cattle or sheep. A few big companies mined gold and silver with machines. In Denver, people opened small stores to sell supplies to the farmers, ranchers, and miners.

A stagecoach company was started. Telegraph wires carried messages over the prairies and plains. Newspapers were published, too. Denver, between the towns on the prairies and the towns in the Rockies, became a meeting place for people and things and ideas.

On the Atlantic Coast, cities grew larger. On the Pacific Coast, cities grew, too. Between them stood the high Rockies, blocking the passage of people, things, and ideas. Many peaks in the Rockies are almost three miles high. Only a few passes cut through these high mountains.

Then came the railroads, stretching across the nation. The first one cut through the Rockies north of Denver. Denver got busy and built a railroad north to the main line. Then the city built railroads south to Mexico and west to the mining towns in the mountains.

Later a tunnel was dug right through the Rockies, and Denver got a main railroad line of its own. It went east to the Atlantic and west to the Pacific. Wheat, cattle, shoes, and sugar could be shipped both east and west. Denver was a railroad center at the edge of the prairie where it meets the mountains.

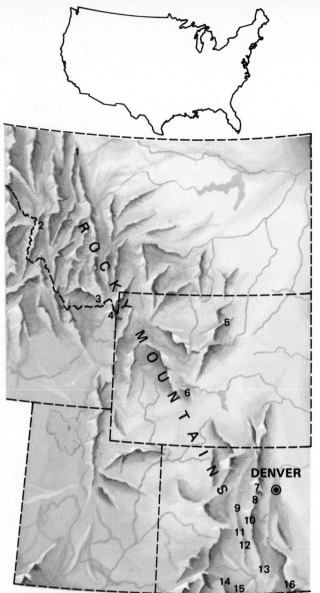

1. Marias Pass	9. Tennessee Pass
2. Lolo Pass	10. Trout Creek Pass
3. Monida Pass	11. Monarch Pass
4. Gore Pass	12. Poncha Pass
5. Powder River Pass	13. La Veta Pass
6. South Pass	14. Wolf Creek Pass
7. Berthoud Pass	15. Cumbres Pass
8. Loveland Pass	16. Raton Pass

Even later, tourists came over the roads in automobiles to Colorado. They fished the clear rivers, hiked in the meadows and mountains, and camped in the national parks.

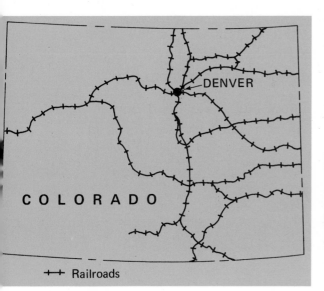

Railroads

Today Denver is a big city, and still growing. From Denver, roads, railroads, and air routes reach all across the land.

Chicago

MOVING WEST

Mary Harper was scared. She had always lived in the East. Tomorrow her family would move from Baltimore to a new city way out West. Her father would be the president of a new university there.

Mary Harper knew that it was wild out West! That night she wrote these words in her diary:

Good-bye, God. We are going to Chicago.

CITY OF CHICAGO,—South-West View, 1845.—Campbell & Co., Printers

Engraved expressly for Norris' Chicago Directory.

MUDDY STREETS

Chicago was a city built on low, **wet** ground where the prairie met Lake Michigan. The streets were wet and muddy. A lot of stories were told about Chicago then. One story told about a man stuck in a mud puddle:

Something had to be done about the mud and water in Chicago. The people decided to build up the streets with dirt. Tons and tons of dirt were used to make every street twelve feet higher. Then the streets of Chicago were high and dry. But every building sat in a deep, wet hole.

The Tremont House was a fine hotel. It was four stories high and made of brick. When the streets of Chicago were built up, the Tremont House was left sitting in a hole.

George Pullman said he could raise the Tremont House without jiggling a single cup or glass in the hotel. First, he got 4,800 jacks. Then he put them under the hotel. He found 1,200 men. Each man gave four jacks one turn. Inch by inch, the building was jacked up. Not a cup or a glass was jiggled. Later, other buildings were lifted, too. That is how Chicago grew twelve feet.

A MIGHTY CITY

Today Chicago is a mighty city. Steel and clothes are made there. Wheat and meat are shipped on trucks, railroads, and boats from Chicago. Ships come from and go to ports all over the world. Chicago's airport is one of the busiest in the United States.

How did Chicago become such a mighty city? Why was it built in such a muddy place? Why did it grow? Part of the answer can be found in maps.

Lake and River Routes

Chicago was built on the edge of Lake Michigan. Lake Michigan is one of the Great Lakes. Look at a map of the United States. See how many places you can reach by traveling on the Great Lakes.

Look at this map of the Mississippi River. It looks like a big tree with branches reaching everywhere. Along every branch, boats can carry goods to build a city. One of those branches reaches right up and almost touches Chicago.

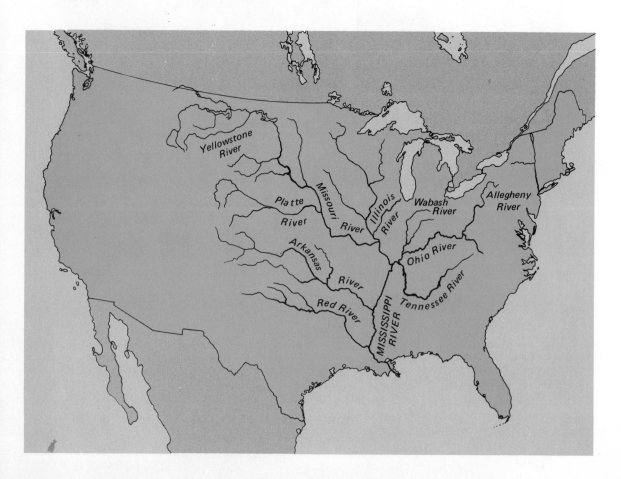

Canal

The Illinois River is a branch of the Mississippi. The people of Chicago had a canal built from Lake Michigan to the Illinois. After that, Chicago stood where riverboats and lake steamers could meet. The first week the canal was open, a riverboat arrived in Chicago. It was bringing sugar to be sent on to Buffalo, New York.

Wheat from Kansas was shipped to Chicago. The city grew. Corn and hogs from Illinois and Iowa were shipped to Chicago. The city grew. Iron came south on the Great Lakes. Coal came north from Illinois. The coal and iron were used to make steel. The city grew.

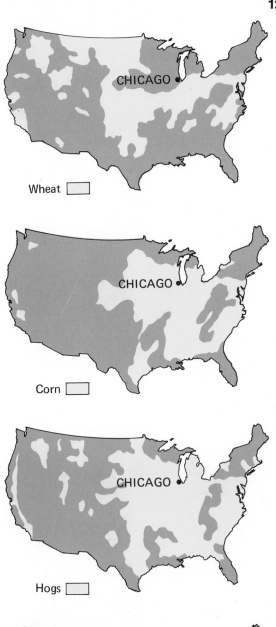

Wheat

Corn

Hogs

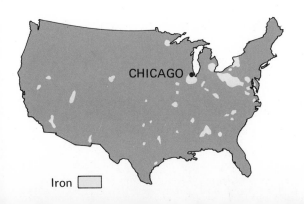

Iron

Coal

Railroads

Later, railroads were built. Chicago became the railroad center for the middle of the United States. Furniture, farm machinery, and clothes were made in Chicago and shipped out by railroad. The city grew.

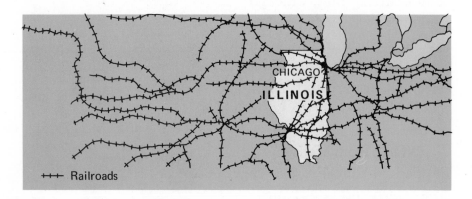

+++ Railroads

Seaway

When the St. Lawrence Seaway was built, ocean ships could come into the port of Chicago. The city grew.

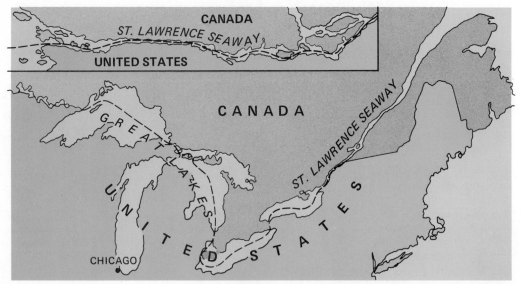

Today Chicago is a mighty city. Its trade routes reach out to the whole world.

New York

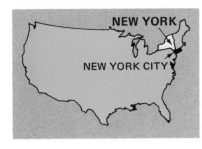

NEW YORK

NEW YORK CITY

THE ISLAND WILL SINK!

This is the day. At last. Manhattan is saved. Hooray!

Everyone in the streets on Manhattan island waited for two men who had a plan.

Oh, when will they get here?

Hurry. The island will sink for sure. Look at all the tall buildings down on the tip. The island will sink for sure!

Oh, when will they come?

"We'll cut Manhattan island off from the mainland. We'll row the island out to sea. We'll turn her around and row her back in. Then we'll pull the heavy end up on the mainland. Manhattan island will be saved from sinking."

This was the plan the two men had. Oh, when will they get here?

All around Manhattan the two men had walked, telling their plan. They asked people to make saws to cut the island loose. Saws 100 feet long. They asked the people to make oars to row the island with. Oars 250 feet long.

Oh, when will they come?

Of course they never came.

Over in Brooklyn, two men from Manhattan laughed and laughed. And the island never sank.

A WORLD OF WATER

The island of Manhattan is part of New York City. It is an island of solid rock. On the island are the high skyscrapers of a great city. Around Manhattan are the other parts of New York City—Brooklyn, Queens, the Bronx, and Staten Island. All these parts make up the city of New York.

New York is on the edge of the Atlantic Ocean. Ships can sail from New York out on to the Atlantic and then to ports around the world. New York is a world of water.

In the harbor of New York are many fine places for ships to dock. Along the Hudson River, ships can dock. Along the East River, ships can dock. Ships can dock at the piers of Brooklyn. New York is a world of water.

Down the Hudson River come barges, flatboats, and ships carrying products from the land west of New York. Down the river come goods to build a city. New York is a world of water.

Erie Canal

Ships will not come into a harbor if no one will buy the goods they bring in. Ships will not sail out if no one has goods to sell. A great port must take goods brought in and give goods to ship out. Long ago, a canal helped New York become a great port.

The Mohawk Valley is like an open door to the Great Lakes. Through this door, timber from Michigan could pass into the port of New York. Through this door, coal, cattle, animal hides, and corn from Illinois and Iowa and Kansas and Nebraska could be shipped to New York.

Back through the door could go the stoves, clothes, furniture, and blankets from New York for the city people and the farm people in Ohio, Michigan, and the other states to the west.

A WATER ROUTE FROM NEW YORK TO THE GREAT LAKES

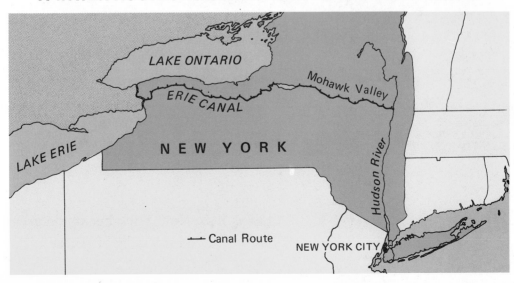

LAKE ONTARIO

Mohawk Valley

ERIE CANAL

LAKE ERIE

N E W   Y O R K

Hudson River

—— Canal Route   NEW YORK CITY

So, the Erie Canal was built in the Mohawk Valley. It connected Lake Erie with the Hudson River. Then goods from the Great Lakes came down the Erie Canal and down the Hudson River to New York. Back up the river and back up the canal to the Great Lakes went goods from New York.

That is how New York became a great port. New York is a world of water.

4

Cities from the
Inside Out

Like Doughnuts and Targets

EXPLAINING BY PRETENDING

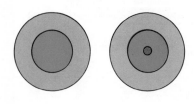

Sometimes people explain one thing by saying it is like something else. Probably you do that yourself.

If you were trying to tell your little brother what a lion is, you could say that it is like your pet cat, only much, much bigger. If you were trying to tell a man from Mars what television is, you could say that it is like the movies, only you watch it at home. He might not know what movies are, but that's another problem.

If you wanted to teach someone what a city is, you could pretend that it is like a big, big doughnut on the land. On a map, you could draw a ring around the edges of a large city. This would make the hole in the doughnut. Then you could draw a ring around all the towns and small cities near the large city. This would make the doughnut.

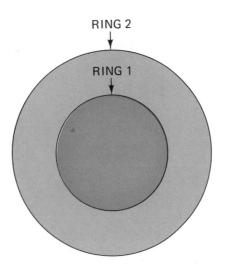

RING 1 shows the edges of the city. Inside RING 1 is the central city. It is the hole in the doughnut. If you walk across the central city, you cannot see the edges. If you fly above it in a plane, you cannot see the edges. RING 1 is a line on a map. It shows the edges of the city.

RING 2 goes around the towns and small cities near the central city. The towns and small cities are the suburbs of the central city. The suburbs are the doughnut. RING 2 is also a line on a map. It shows the edges of the towns and small cities near the central city.

If you drew a doughnut map of a city, it might look like this.

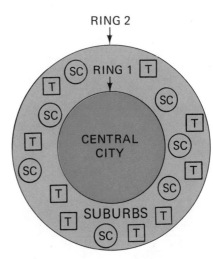

T Town   SC Small City

Worcester Is Like a Doughnut

This picture shows part of the city doughnut of Worcester, Massachusetts. The white solid line is RING 1, the edges of the central city. Inside RING 1 is the central city of Worcester, the hole in the doughnut.

The white dotted line is RING 2, the edges of the towns and small cities. Inside RING 2 are the suburbs of Worcester, the doughnut.

THE HOLE IN
THE HOLE IN THE DOUGHNUT

Inside the central city is a place where many buildings bunch together. They reach up high into the sky. Inside these skyscrapers are banks, stores, and business offices.

You can draw RING 3 around this place where the tall buildings crowd together. RING 3 makes the hole in the hole in the doughnut.

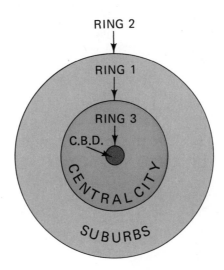

Now your doughnut looks like a target. RING 3 looks like the bull's-eye on the target. Geographers have a special name for RING 3. They call it the Central Business District, or the C.B.D. When you are going to the C.B.D., you probably say you are "going downtown" or "going into town" or "going to the city."

The Hole in the Hole in Spokane

Look at this picture of Spokane, Washington. Do you see a place with many tall buildings? That place is the C.B.D. of Spokane. That is the hole in the hole in Spokane.

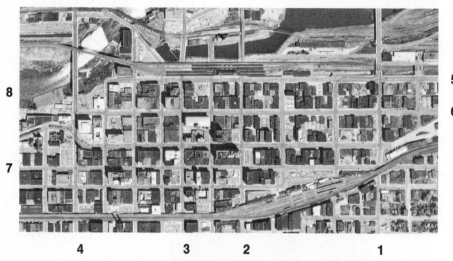

Now look at the map of Spokane. Can you find the C.B.D. on the map?

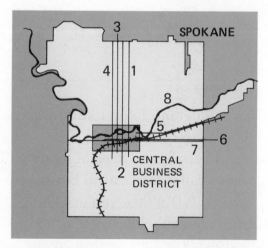

Look hard at the picture of Spokane. Is there a river on one side of the tall buildings? Which streets are near the tall buildings? These hints will help you find the C.B.D. in Spokane. Use your finger to trace RING 3 on the map.

1. Division St.
2. Washington St.
3. Howard St.
4. Monroe St.
5. Trent Ave.
6. Riverside Ave.
7. Sprague St.
8. *Spokane River*

All About the C.B.D.

THE C.B.D. LONG AGO

If you go to a city, you can tell where the C.B.D. is. The C.B.D. is the place where many tall buildings are squeezed tightly together. When you stand on the sidewalk and look up, sometimes you cannot see the tops of the skyscrapers. Some are so tall their tops are lost in the clouds.

Long ago, the C.B.D. was the busiest place in the city, just as it is today. But it looked very very different then. A blacksmith's shop might have stood where today you see a garage. As you walked along, you would pass a post office, a general store, and a drugstore. On windy days, the hanging signs creaked outside the small banks and hotels and shops.

Make believe you are living long ago, when your great-grandparents were children. Pretend you are going to visit the C.B.D. long ago.

It is hard to get to the C.B.D., and it takes a long time. It might even take half a day. If you come from a farm, you can ride in your wagon. If you are rich, you can ride downtown in a fancy rig pulled by high-stepping horses. But if you are poor, you may have to walk all the way.

Once you are in the C.B.D., you can shop for all kinds of things you cannot find at home. You can buy a hat that was made in a factory and wear it instead of your knitted hat. You can buy a newspaper, shiny boots, or salt for the dinner table.

Cincinnati

New York City

The C.B.D. was an exciting place if you lived on a farm or in a village. Maybe it wasn't much compared with the C.B.D. today. Still, it was where the business world lived. Goods were bought and sold there. Horses clip-clopped along brick streets. You did not hear the screeching brakes and loud horns of cars. But you did hear the neighs of horses and the squeaking of wagon wheels. People called back and forth to each other. Noises and voices and dust filled the air.

But the C.B.D. did not stay small. By the time your great-grandparents were grown up, it had changed. The C.B.D. changed from a low, dusty place to a place of tall buildings tightly packed together. Skyscrapers and concrete covered the ground. How did it happen?

Sacramento

Baltimore

STREETCARS CHANGED THE C.B.D.

Horsecars

When the first cities were built in the United States, people walked to work in the C.B.D. After work, they walked home again. Walking was slow, so they lived close to their offices and stores. They could live only one or two miles away.

Then someone built a horse carriage big enough to carry twenty people. He called it the horsecar. The horsecar ran on two rails in the middle of the street. Two horses pulled it along the rails. Everybody paid a nickel to ride downtown. People could live four miles from the C.B.D. and still get to work on time.

A ride in a horsecar was faster than walking, but it was still slow. A horsecar could go only six miles an hour on flat ground. Besides, each horse cost $200. A horse could work for only three or four years. And each car needed three or four pairs of horses because each pair could work only four hours a day.

The horses in San Francisco had to pull the cars up very steep hills. It was hard, slow work. So Andrew Hallidie invented the cable car. The cable car was attached to a steam-powered cable running in a slot in the street. The cable pulled the car about nine miles an hour up and down the steep hills.

Cable Cars

Andrew Smith Hallidie
1836 - 1900
Inventor of the Cable Street Railway

Fifteen cities put in cable cars. Chicago had 710! But sometimes a car came off its cable. Then all the people had to climb out and push the car back into place.

Trolley Cars

Frank Sprague built an electric streetcar for Richmond, Virginia. His streetcar also ran along tracks in the street. But electricity made it move. A small four-wheeled "trolley" on top of the car rode along two overhead electric wires. Naturally, the new streetcar was called the trolley car.

Trolley cars were speedy and cheap to run. They never needed to rest, and they didn't come off their tracks.

Cities laid trolley car lines farther and farther away from the C.B.D. People in the central city followed the lines to the suburbs. They built houses farther and farther away from the city, along the trolley car lines. They could ride the trolley cars to their jobs in the C.B.D. Cities began to grow long fingers out into the country, far from the C.B.D.

HOW THE C.B.D. CHANGED

The streetcar was the first invention that changed the C.B.D. What did it do?

Business people and shopkeepers all wanted to be in the C.B.D. They wanted to be where the streetcars came together downtown. The price of land went up and up. And the factory owners who needed more land for new buildings had to move out. They sold their valuable C.B.D. land to the business people and shopkeepers.

In a few years, offices, stores, banks, theaters, and restaurants had bought up nearly all the land in the C.B.D. Buildings were jammed together. Almost the only space left was on the streets.

More and more people kept coming to the C.B.D. in streetcars. They came to work, and they came to shop. The stores and offices needed still more room to grow. But the little land that was left was very costly.

The C.B.D. could grow only one way—**UP!**

SKYSCRAPERS CHANGED THE C.B.D.

If storekeepers wanted their C.B.D. stores to grow, all they had to do was add another floor. By building the stores higher, storekeepers could keep adding to their stores without buying more land.

Buildings in the C.B.D. began to grow up. They grew taller and taller, until they were four or five stories high. And there they stopped.

The buildings stopped growing because the walls were made of bricks. The bricks on the bottom had to hold up all the bricks above them, and every floor. So the bottom of the walls had to be very strong. The way to make them very strong was to use many bricks to make them very thick. But thick walls used up too much land at the bottoms of the buildings. If people wanted buildings taller than four or five stories, they would have to find another way to build them.

William Jenney found the way. He built a steel frame, like this, in Chicago.

The steel frame was ten stories tall. It could hold up the walls and the floors of a building, in the same way your skeleton holds up your body. You don't need great big feet to hold you up. Even a full-grown fat man doesn't need bigger feet than a full-grown skinny man. A very tall building with a strong steel frame doesn't need walls that are very thick at the bottom to hold it up.

After Jenney finished the building, it looked like this.

Making buildings with steel skeletons was a good idea. The buildings in the C.B.D. could reach higher and higher. They could touch the sky. People could build skyscrapers. The steel frame skyscraper was the second invention that changed the C.B.D.

ELECTRIC ELEVATORS CHANGED THE C.B.D.

To grow up, the C.B.D. really needed two things. One was a new way to make taller buildings. The other was a new kind of elevator to carry people up and down the taller buildings.

The old-time elevators were slow and not very safe. They were used to carry sacks and boxes. People never rode in them. They walked up the stairs and then down again.

No one minded walking up one or two flights of wooden stairs in the old C.B.D. buildings to get a tooth filled. Three flights weren't too many to buy a cotton dress. Even four flights were all right, unless you had to carry a heavy package. But nobody would walk up ten flights of stairs!

Faster and safer elevators were needed to carry people up to and down from the offices and shops in the new skyscrapers. Inventors quickly went to work.

The first electric elevator was soon put into a building in New York City. It was safe. It was quick. It could carry many people.

The electric elevator solved a hard problem. Buildings could grow taller and taller—twenty stories—fifty stories—a hundred stories. The C.B.D. grew up and up. The electric elevator was the third invention that changed the C.B.D.

THE C.B.D. TODAY

Remember how you pretended you were in the C.B.D. long ago, when your great-grandparents were children? Now pretend you are walking in the C.B.D. today.

It is early morning. It is quiet. The morning sounds you hear at home are not here. The sun slants down between the tall buildings. If you walk on one side of the street, the sun lights up the store fronts. If you cross to the other side, the skyscrapers stand in their own shadows.

What a difference if you walk in the C.B.D. at noon. People with briefcases jostle each other on the crowded sidewalks. Shoes go click, click, click. Cars and honking trucks fill the streets. Signs light up, snap off, light up, snap off. Inside the buildings are all the buzzing, clacking, hurrying noises of people hard at work.

Then pretend you are in the C.B.D. at sunset. Lights pop on in all the windows. First one and then another, until the sky above you blazes with squares of light.

Soon the lights begin to go out in the offices and stores. First one and then another. People are leaving work to go to their apartments in other parts of the central city. Some are leaving the C.B.D. to go to their homes in the suburbs.

After midnight, the C.B.D. is dark and nearly empty. A night watchman whistles a tune. A policeman's footsteps echo in the quiet air. A street cleaning truck swooshes by.

Why do people come to the C.B.D.? They come to work in the tall buildings. They come to shop and to eat in the restaurants and to go to plays.

Most of them live somewhere else. Few people live in the C.B.D. today.

Population and Density

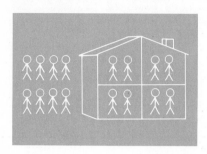

Have you ever held a mixing bowl full of cake batter? If you tip the bowl to one side, all the batter rolls that way. If you tip it to the other side, the batter rolls that way. When you put the bowl down flat again, the batter settles back in the middle.

A city full of people is something like a bowl full of cake batter. All day, hundreds of thousands of people move around in the city as if it were a giant bowl tipping back and forth. But usually the people go back to where they started from. They go back to where they live and sleep.

How do you find out how many people a city has? You do not count the people at work in the C.B.D. or at school or at the circus. You count them where they live and sleep.

When you count the number of people who live in a city, you are counting the population of the city. When you count the number of people in a suburb, you are counting the population of the suburb. You can even count the population of one house. Population is the number of people who live in a place.

POPULATION IS A NUMBER

DENSITY IS A NUMBER AND SPACE

If you count the number of people who live in a city, you are counting its population. But if you count the number of people who live in a city and then figure out how much space they live in, you are thinking about density. Density is the number of people who live in a certain amount of space.

Pretend your classroom is a city. If there are 28 children in your class, and a teacher and an aide, the population of your classroom is 30.

Everybody can probably move around comfortably in your classroom city. Each person has enough space to work. That means the density is low.

But if you invite another third-grade class to move into your classroom city, you would have to fit many more people into the same space. Each person would have less space. The density of your classroom city would be high.

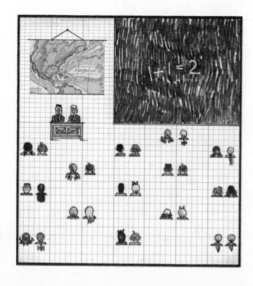
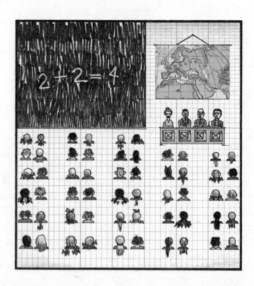

THEY ARE NOT THE SAME

A city can have many, many people—a large population—and still have a low density. Phoenix has many, many people. But it is a wide, spread-out city. It has a large population, but it has a low density. Low density means that many people live in a big space.

San Francisco has a large population, like Phoenix. But the people of San Francisco have little space to live in. San Francisco has a large population and a high density. High density means that many people live in a small space.

PHOENIX, ARIZONA

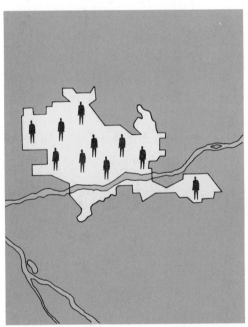

SAN FRANCISCO, CALIFORNIA

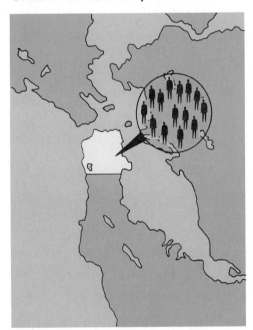

Key 👤 = 50,000 People

Compare the map of Phoenix with the map of San Francisco. Can you see why Phoenix has a low density and San Francisco has a high density?

Three City Families

Cities are like one another in some ways. Paterson in New Jersey, St. Louis in Missouri, and Portland in Oregon are all cities. They have central city areas with C.B.D.'s. Around their edges are many suburbs.

Cities are different from one another in some ways. Paterson is a doughnut that overlaps many other doughnuts near New York City. St. Louis is a lopsided doughnut because it lies beside the great Mississippi River. Portland is a doughnut filled with green patches of lawn and trees. Except in the C.B.D., it is hard to tell whether you are in the central city or in the suburbs.

Here are pictures of these three cities. How are they alike? How are they different?

Paterson

Portland

St. Louis

THE RAMOS FAMILY

Pedro Ramos lives in Paterson. He is in the third grade. He lives with his parents and his older sister, Antonia. Antonia is in the eighth grade. The family came to Paterson just three years ago from Puerto Rico.

Pedro and his family live in an apartment near the C.B.D. The apartment is pleasant and bright. Sometimes Pedro can hear the sounds of the busy streets nearby.

Look at the map of Paterson below. Where is the C.B.D.? Where is the central city? Where are the suburbs? Can you find Pedro's apartment? How far does Pedro live from the central city? If Pedro wanted to go to the nearest park, how far would he have to go? How could he get there?

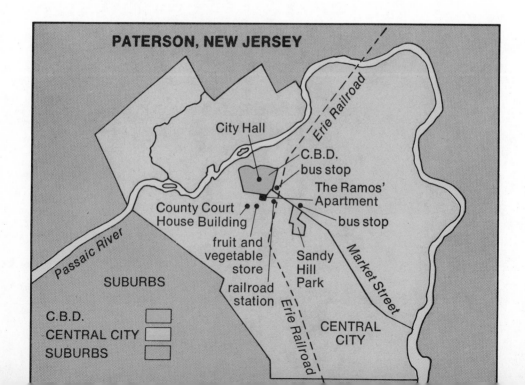

Pedro lives in this building. What can you tell about Pedro's home? How is it like yours? How is it different? What can you tell about Pedro's neighborhood from these pictures?

Mr. Ramos works as a bookkeeper for a furniture factory. He usually takes a bus to work each day, but on nice days he likes to walk. He is glad that his office is not far from his home.

Mrs. Ramos does not work at another job. She makes a home for her family. She cooks, cleans, and sews. Sometimes she helps Pedro with his school work. She is very busy.

Almost every day Pedro goes to the fruit and vegetable store nearby. The family likes to eat fresh vegetables every day. Once a week, they take a bus to the supermarket.

Pedro's family does not have a car. The streets are crowded, and a car would be hard to park. Besides, buses and trains go almost everywhere.

In the evening Pedro and his family like to spend time together. Sometimes they watch television. Sometimes after dinner they go for a walk. They often stop to watch the soccer game in the park nearby.

Pedro likes to go to school. His favorite classes are arithmetic and music. Pedro's father has a calculator that Pedro has learned to use. He can add and subtract on it.

After school, Pedro usually plays in the park with his friends. Sometimes he goes to the Boys' Club. He can swim there or play many different games. He can also make things in the arts and crafts workshop. He made Antonia a leather belt for her birthday.

One time Pedro and some of his friends went to New York on the bus. They saw the New York Rangers play hockey. It was very exciting!

Pedro would like to visit Puerto Rico again some day. He could stay with his grandparents who still live there. His parents have promised him that he can go when he is ten years old.

THE STEIN FAMILY

Natalie Stein lives in Portland with her mother, her grandfather, her brother, Mark, and her sister, Debbie. Mark is in kindergarten and Debbie is only four, so Natalie, who is eight, is the oldest.

The Stein family lives in a house with a small yard. It is on a quiet street with trees and lawns. But Natalie and her family still live in the city.

Look at the map of Portland below. Can you find where Natalie lives? How far does Natalie live from the C.B.D.? What do you call the part of the city where Natalie lives? Where might Natalie go to play?

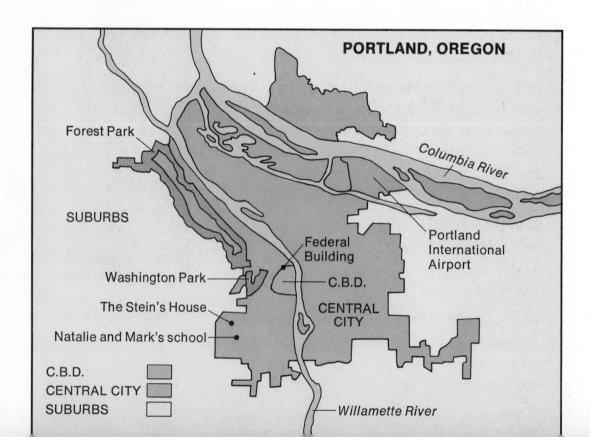

Natalie lives in this house. How is her house like yours? How is it different? What can you tell about Natalie's neighborhood from these pictures?

Natalie's grandfather is very important to the family. In the morning he makes breakfast for everybody. Debbie doesn't go to school yet so he takes care of her during the day. Sometimes he bakes special surprises for Natalie and Mark when they come home from school. Natalie's favorite is chocolate chip cookies.

Mrs. Stein works at Electek, a local factory. She is an engineer. The Stein family has a car, but Mrs. Stein does not drive it every day. She rides in a car pool so she only has to drive to work one day a week.

Natalie takes the school bus every morning. Her school is old, but the rooms are brightly painted and the playground is big. Natalie's favorite time of the day is gym class. She likes sports, especially softball and basketball. She and her mother sometimes shoot baskets.

One weekend Natalie and her mother went to see the Portland Trailblazers play basketball. It was lots of fun!

Every year, Grandfather Stein takes the children to see the circus. They like to look at all the acts and listen to the band. Natalie likes the clowns best of all.

During the summer, the family goes camping every other weekend. They load the car with their tent and their sleeping bags. Then they drive into the mountains, find a pretty spot, and set up their camp. Natalie likes to collect leaves from the trees near camp. Then she and her grandfather look up what kind of tree each leaf is from.

Each Wednesday after school, Natalie goes to Brownie meetings. They learn songs and games, and they make things, too. Natalie is making a scrapbook of the leaves that she collected on her camping trips.

Natalie likes living in Portland. She is happy that her family does many different things together.

¹⁶² THE MAGEE FAMILY

Arthur Magee lives in University City with his parents, his two brothers, and his sister. Arthur is in the third grade. His sister, Gloria, is in high school. The twins, Michael and Steven, are six.

Their modern ranch house is filled with all the members of their family. But the yard is big. Arthur likes to play here with his friends. In the summer the family sometimes barbecues in their yard.

Look at this map of St. Louis. Where is University City? Where is Arthur's house? Is it in the C.B.D., the central city, or the suburbs? How far does Arthur live from the Mississippi River? How far does he live from the C.B.D.? Where is the park closest to Arthur's house? How would he get there?

Arthur lives in this house with his family.
How is it like yours? How is it different?
Look at the pictures carefully. What can you
tell about Arthur's neighborhood?

Mr. Magee is a foreman at an automobile factory where he has worked for many years. He drives his car to work every day because there is little bus service in University City.

Without a car, Mrs. Magee has a hard time getting to her job. She is thinking about buying a car of her own. Mrs. Magee works two days a week at the art museum. Sometimes she visits schools and talks about art. She talked to Arthur's third grade class one afternoon. He felt very proud of his mother!

Arthur often visits his mother at the museum. His favorite class at school is art. He likes to draw or paint pictures at home, too. He hangs the ones he likes the best around his room.

On Tuesday afternoons Arthur goes to Cub Scout meetings. Sometimes the troop goes on special trips. Last fall they went to see the St. Louis Cardinals play football.

On most other afternoons Arthur plays with his friends. Twice a year he and his friends camp out overnight in somebody's backyard. They cook hot dogs and marshmallows and tell ghost stories.

On Sundays the family often goes to Forest Park. They like to visit the zoo there. If the weather is good, they bring a picnic along. Arthur sometimes gives part of his lunch to the elephants.

Arthur and his friend Lois love boats. Whenever they can, they go to the Mississippi River. There they spend hours watching the boats go up and down.

CITIES FROM THE INSIDE OUT

Cities are big places. Parts of cities are different from one another. Every city is different from every other city. That is why cities are so exciting.

More people live in city doughnuts than in the places outside the doughnuts. In this country, most people live in cities. Soon, 8 out of every 10 Americans will live in cities.

A city grows outward in rings, from the C.B.D. to the suburbs. In most of the rings, families like the Ramos family and the Stein family and the Magee family work and play and go to school and try to have the best life they can.

5

Where Are the Edges?

Last Ring Around the City

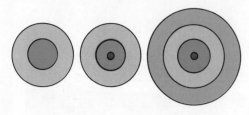

Do you remember how you pretended a city is like a doughnut? You drew a map of the central city and suburbs, like this:

Then you added another ring inside the central city. This ring marked off the C.B.D. The doughnut became a target with a bull's-eye, like this:

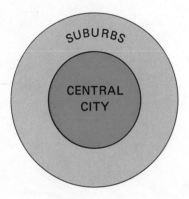

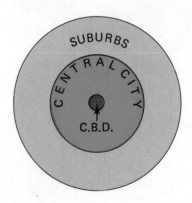

ONE MORE RING

Do you live in a city? in the suburbs of a city? Do you know what lies beyond the suburbs?

Do you live in the country? in a desert? high on a mountain? To show these places, your target map needs one more ring. It is the ring beyond the city and the suburbs. Another word for this ring is hinterlands.

HINTERLANDS ARE SPECIAL

How do you know if you're in the hinterlands?

You are riding along in a car. How will you know when you get to the hinterlands? Well, for one thing, the further you go from the city, the fewer buildings you see. Soon, there are miles and miles of land with no buildings at all. It is quiet. When night comes, you see only a few lights. These are clues that tell you you're in the hinterlands.

You see other changes, too. City stores are often big and busy. People crowd in and out the doors. They want to buy things and hurry on.

But a hinterlands store is usually a small building. One person can serve everybody. Shopkeepers in the hinterlands know most of their customers. They can call them by name and know where they live. Sometimes people come to a hinterlands store just to sit and chat with their neighbors.

In the city, letter-carriers walk to
each house and apartment building,
carrying the mail. In the hinterlands, they
drive from mailbox to mailbox along
the roads.

On each hinterlands mailbox is a flag.
If the flag is up, the letter-carrier stops and
takes the letters out of the box. Today's
mail is put into the box and the flag is left
up. If there is no mail for the family that
day, the letter-carrier pushes the flag down.
From the house, the family can look out a
window. When the mailbox flag is up,
someone walks to the road to see what
came in the mail.

Mapping the Hinterlands

Some scientists say you can tell the hinterlands of a city if you know what newspaper most of the people read. Sometimes the mailboxes give you that clue. Many newspaper companies send free mailboxes to their customers. The names of the newspapers are written in big letters on these mailboxes.

GREATVILLE AND WORLDTOWN

Pretend you are studying two cities that are three hundred miles apart. One is called Greatville, and the other is called Worldtown. How could you figure out where to draw the last ring around Greatville?

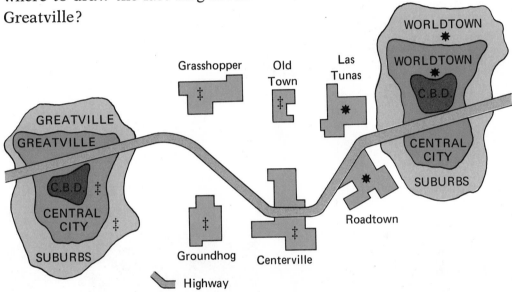

If most people in a town read the *Greatville News*, then that town is in the hinterlands of Greatville. Look at the map key. What newspaper do most people read in each town? Now you can figure out where to draw the last ring around Greatville.

LOOKING FOR OTHER CLUES

Some hinterlands are deserts. Joshua trees stand with crooked arms in the desert hinterlands.

Some hinterlands are rocky coasts.

Some hinterlands are high mountains.

Others are flat, bare places where there is nothing to hide behind.

The hinterlands of some cities are patches of green fields and black, wet earth. Wheat and cornstalks wave in the hot sun and bend under the summer rain.

Other hinterlands are hot and dusty places. The dryness hurts your nose.

Each hinterland is different. But you can always tell when you're in the hinterlands if you look for the clues.

Taking a Walk

The hinterlands have very few sidewalks. Wire fences run down long roads. As you walk the roads, the wind often hits you in the face. At night, the roads are very dark unless the moon is up. The yellow squares of light in the farmhouse windows seem far away.

When you reach a town, you see sidewalks and trees along the streets. You can smell newly mowed lawns. On Main Street, people are coming out of the movies. They call to each other saying goodnight. Cars start up and turn the corner to head for home. One by one, the lights around town go out.

Taking a Ride

When you walk in the hinterlands, telephone poles seem very far apart. But when you ride in a car, the poles flash by. There are no traffic jams. Sometimes your car is the only one on the road.

Long ago, people in the mountain hinterlands put bells on their wagons. That way, other wagon drivers could hear them coming around the mountain roads. Today, people in the mountain hinterlands toot their car horns as they drive around the sharp turns.

Long ago, horses pulling wagons up steep hinterlands hills never stopped. If the horses stopped, they might never get going again. Today, people driving down these steep, narrow roads turn off and stop when they see cars coming up the hills. That way, the cars can chug right to the top without stopping.

Looking Down

From a plane, high above, hinterlands often look like checkerboards. The squares on the ground are fields of cotton, corn, or wheat. Sometimes the squares are woods. Roads, fences, and telephone lines cut the land into pieces.

At night in a plane, the sky is sprinkled with stars beside you and above you. Down below, the lights of the hinterland towns look like diamonds spread across the land. You can sometimes see the soft glow of a city faraway.

Hinterlands, U.S.A.

The United States is a big country. It stretches from Alaska to Maine. It reaches from North Dakota to the tip of Texas. It spreads from Georgia to California, and on across the Pacific Ocean to Hawaii. Each state has its cities and their hinterlands. All are different, but they are all alike. Every city reaches out to its hinterlands. Each small town reaches toward its city.

Pretend you are taking a trip around the United States. You will visit six cities and their hinterlands. How are they different? How are they alike?

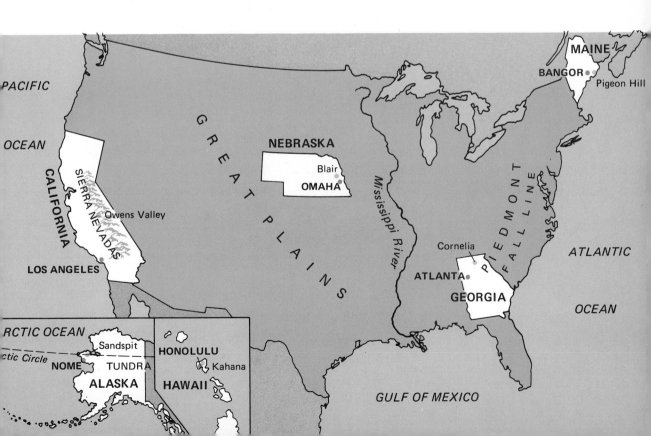

BANGOR, MAINE

Bangor is one of the biggest cities in the state of Maine. In the hinterlands of Bangor are mountain forests and fields of potatoes.

South and east of Bangor is the Atlantic Ocean and the coast hinterlands. The long, rocky shore is uneven and ragged. It goes up and down and in and out. Many islands dot the bays along the shore.

This part of Maine is called a drowned coastline. The islands were once the tops of mountains. That was millions of years ago, before the glaciers came.

Along the drowned coastline, peninsulas stick out into the ocean like long rocky fingers. On one peninsula is the village of Pigeon Hill. The people there fish for lobsters and clams. They dry their lobster traps in the sun along the bay.

The lobsters and clams are sent to Bangor. From Bangor, the fish is shipped to cities all over the world.

Pigeon Hill has no store and no gas station. Its people go to Bangor to buy groceries for their kitchens and gas for their boat engines. Pigeon Hill people read the *Bangor News.* Pigeon Hill is in the hinterlands of Bangor.

ATLANTA, GEORGIA

Back from the Atlantic Ocean toward the faraway mountains is the Piedmont of Georgia. The Piedmont is a wide table, or plateau, of hard rock. Rich farmlands lie on top of the hard rock. The good soils have washed down from the mountains for many thousands of years.

The hard rock ends suddenly at the eastern and southern edges of the Piedmont. The place where the wide table of hard rock ends is called the Fall Line. Rivers, coming to this sharp drop, turn into waterfalls and rapids. The falling water is used to make electric power for factories.

Rich farmlands and falling water for power make a good place for cities to grow.

Atlanta, Georgia, is one of the Fall Line cities.

North and east of Atlanta is the tiny town
of Cornelia. Short winters, long summers,
and rich soil washed down the mountains
onto the Piedmont mean good farming
in Cornelia.

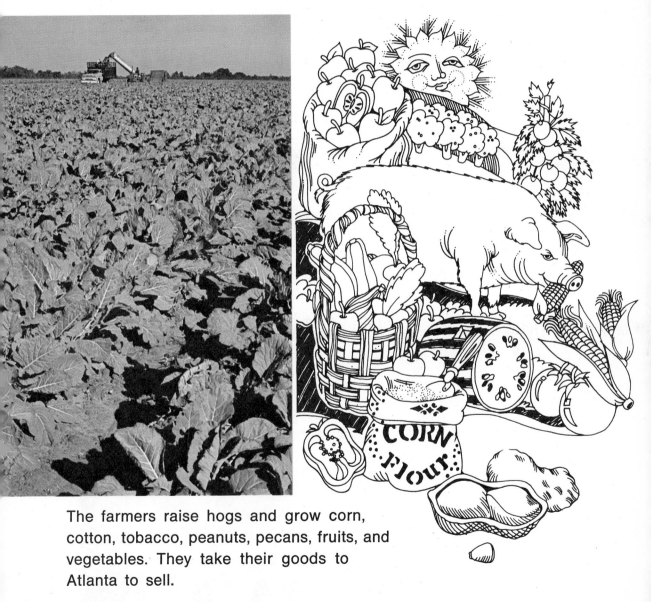

The farmers raise hogs and grow corn,
cotton, tobacco, peanuts, pecans, fruits, and
vegetables. They take their goods to
Atlanta to sell.

Cornelia is in the hinterlands of Atlanta.

OMAHA, NEBRASKA

Westward ho!

From Georgia, you travel west to the Great Plains. This is the biggest plain in North America. It stretches 3,000 miles, from the Gulf of Mexico to the Arctic Ocean, up near the North Pole.

Omaha, Nebraska, is a city on the Great Plains. The land around Omaha is flat, flat, flat. Railroad tracks and highways run smooth and straight across Nebraska.

Did you ever eat a TV dinner? Omaha makes and ships more TV dinners than any other city in the world.

On the rich plain around Omaha, the corn grows tall. It is feed corn, for cattle. Omaha is the center for a large hinterlands where beef cattle are raised.

Blair is a cattle town in the hinterlands of Omaha. Omaha needs Blair and the other hinterlands towns around it to be a great city.

The ranchers and farmers in Blair need Omaha, too. They sell their goods in the city and shop in the city stores.

LOS ANGELES, CALIFORNIA

Now you will go to the hot, dry land around Los Angeles, California.

More than sixty years ago, people in Los Angeles began to look far and wide for water. The city was growing. It needed water to grow even faster. The people of Los Angeles bought the land in the Owens Valley.

The Owens Valley is a high desert valley. But it lies behind the Sierra Nevadas. Deep creeks and streams run down into the valley from the mountains.

The Owens Valley is a long way from Los Angeles. Yet it is in the hinterlands of the city. The people from Los Angeles ran great pipes to their city. The cold mountain water sped through the pipes to Los Angeles. The Owens Valley is in the hinterlands of Los Angeles because its water goes to the city.

But the farmers of the Owens Valley needed the water! Without the water, they could not farm. Their land dried up. Houses fell into ruin. Today, the Owens Valley is mostly dry and brown.

HONOLULU, HAWAII

Hawaii is the newest state. It lies on islands in the blue Pacific. Volcanoes formed these islands. The volcano mountains grew higher and higher up out of the ocean. The lava from the bursting volcanoes grew hard and made new mountains. They were shaped like upside-down ice-cream-cones.

The upside-down ice-cream-cone mountains burst open again and again. The volcanoes spit out more lava, and the lava formed still more mountains.

This went on for millions of years. It is still going on.

On the island of Oahu is the largest city in Hawaii. It is Honolulu. Airplanes and ships bring thousands of visitors to Honolulu every year.

Most of Oahu is rock. Fruits and vegetables can grow only on a small part of the island. Pineapple is one of those fruits.

The pineapple fields are in the hinterlands of Honolulu. Kahana is one of the hinterland towns.

Many people of Kahana work in the pineapple fields. Others work in a factory near the fields. Here the pineapple is canned or made into juice. Then the fruit and juice are sent to Honolulu. From there, they are shipped to cities all over the world.

NOME, ALASKA

Now you start on the last part of your trip—north toward the Arctic Circle.

Nome, Alaska, is a city near the Arctic Circle. It is a modern city. Cars and trucks move in and out on highways built over deep swamps, fast rivers, and high mountains. Small seaplanes fly from the city to lakes in the hinterlands. The planes carry mail and food and medicine.

East of Nome is the frozen tundra. The tundra is frozen solid for ten months of the year. Only a few plants, like moss and very small trees, grow there. Only a few animals, like caribou, reindeer, wolves, and foxes, live there.

In the winter, the tundra is like a frozen desert. When the short summer comes, the top few inches of the tundra soil grow soft. Grass and tiny flowers pop through the ground. But, underneath, the tundra never melts.

Most people do not think that the tundra is a good place to live. The winter is almost too cold. The summer air is filled with mosquitoes and black flies. That is why Sandspit is a tiny town.

The people of Sandspit are born in the hospital in Nome. They go to the doctors in Nome when they are sick. They shop there, too. They go to the city to find work.

Cities Without Edges

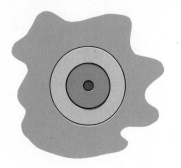

CHOCOLATE TOWN

Have you ever heard of Hershey, Pennsylvania? Sometimes it is called Chocolate Town. Can you guess why?

Children in Bogota, Colombia, like Hershey bars. Mountain climbers in the Himalayas put Hershey bars into their packs. Taxi drivers in African cities eat Hershey bars for snacks. Farmers in Japan carry Hershey bars with them out to their fields.

In most of the world, people eat Hershey bars. They are living in the hinterlands of Hershey, Pennsylvania.

Do people where you live eat Hershey bars? Do you live in the hinterlands of Chocolate Town?

Where is the last ring around Hershey, Pennsylvania? What are the hinterlands of Chocolate Town?

MEGALOPOLIS

Mega is a Greek word. It means very large. *Polis* is also a Greek word. It means city. Put *mega* and *polis* together, put *lo* between them, and you have megalopolis.

Megalopolis means a very large city. It means a supercity.

Bosnywash

If you travel along the Atlantic Coast, you go from one city to another. The cities have grown out to fill up the space between them.

Look at the map. Bosnywash is the name of a megalopolis. It is a supercity. It spreads from Boston south to Washington. What city in between makes up the middle of this megalopolis?

BOSNYWASH

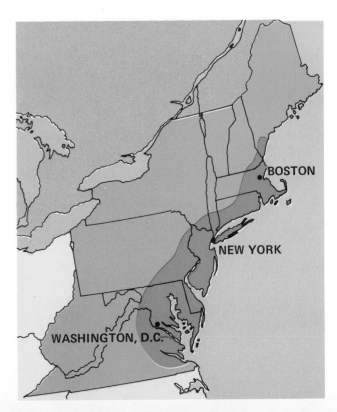

Sanlosdiego

Along the Pacific Ocean, cities are also growing out to fill up the space between them. There are cities from Los Angeles north to Santa Barbara. There are cities from Los Angeles south to San Diego.

There is still some space between the cities along the Pacific Ocean. But every year, the space is less, and the cities are more. Soon the cities might all run together. They will make a megalopolis. It might be called Sanlosdiego.

SANLOSDIEGO

CALIFORNIA

SANTA BARBARA

LOS ANGELES

SAN DIEGO

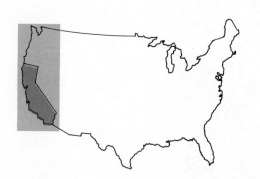

Why are the edges of a city sometimes hard to find? Where are the edges of Bosnywash? Where would you draw the last ring around Sanlosdiego?

Tin Lizzie

Just Imagine!

Just imagine! A land without cars! There would be no highways. No motels. No traffic lights. No parking meters.

If there were no cars, there would be no service stations. No need for gas and oil. No need for tires. No stopping for water. There would be no cars to stop.

Just imagine! A land without cars!

Not so long ago, people went to town
to shop. Some walked to the city. Some
drove wagons. Some rode the streetcars.
A few even took the trains into town.

Today, many people drive their cars
to large shopping centers outside the city.
They park the cars in parking lots.

But not so long ago, there were no shopping centers.

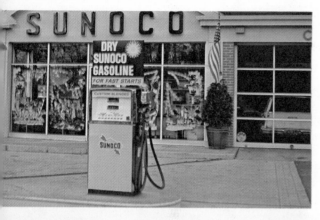

There were no parking lots.
There were no garages, either.
There were no used-car lots.
There were no drive-in banks.
There were no drive-in movies.
There were no drive-in hamburger stands.

There were no cars at all!
Just imagine! A land without cars!

Mr. Fixit

Even when Henry Ford was a small boy, he liked to teach himself how things worked. Sometimes this meant trouble. "Don't let Henry see that toy," said his brothers and sisters. "He'll take it apart."

One year for his birthday, Henry got his own watch. He sat right down and took it all apart. Then he put it back together again. That's how Henry Ford taught himself how the watch worked.

After that, Henry looked high and low for broken watches and clocks. He fixed every one he got his hands on. A neighbor joked about Henry. He said that his clocks started to shake when Henry came near the house. The clocks knew that Mr. Fixit would open them up and poke around inside.

Henry Ford was born into the world of horses and buggies. There were no cars. There were no buses. Everyone used horses or buggies.

One day, Henry and his father hitched their team of horses to the wagon and drove over the plank road to Detroit. There on the road, Henry saw a farm machine chugging along. It was going down the road, from farm to farm, by its own power. The machine had a steam engine.

Before his father could stop their wagon, Henry jumped off. Out popped the questions. "How does it turn?" "How much power does it have?" "What is that thing for?" Henry Ford was teaching himself about a new machine.

Henry went to work in Detroit. In those days, Detroit had twenty miles of streetcar line. Horses pulled the streetcars. Henry rode the streetcars back and forth to work. He thought about a machine that moved by its own power. He thought about a horseless carriage.

All over the land, other people were thinking about a horseless carriage, too.

Two brothers put a gasoline engine on a wagon. They called it a Buggyaut.

Another man put an electric engine on a wagon. He called it an Electrobat.

Henry Ford decided to build his own horseless carriage. He worked all winter making an engine. He fastened it to the kitchen sink. His wife fed gasoline into the engine. It banged, and it smoked. Mr. Fixit was teaching himself how to make a gasoline engine.

At last, the engine worked. Henry put it on a small wagon with bicycle wheels. He started the engine. The wagon moved. Mr. Fixit had built a horseless carriage.

Horseless Carriages

Soon horseless carriages were everywhere.

Some had electric motors.

The Pierce Stanhope

The Woods Electric

Surrey

Style 119
Price $1850
Canopy Top
$100 extra

WOODS MOTOR VEHICLE
COMPANY

Some cars ran on steam power.

The Stanley Steamer

The White Steamer

Others had gasoline motors.

The Franklin

The Sears Motor Buggy

The first cars were big. They cost
a lot of money. Rich people bought them.
Sometimes they paid men to drive the
cars and to keep them running. The
drivers were called chauffeurs. City streets
were soon crowded with big cars driven
by chauffeurs.

People needed special clothes to go driving.

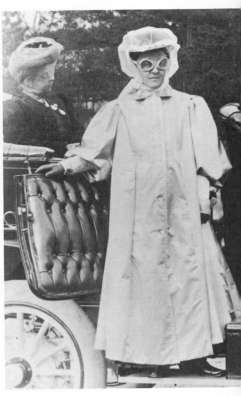

Some people drove their cars on tours.

Everyone wanted a car.

They want it.

They get it.

To the country

Pass a farmer

Scare the horse

Breakdown

Farmer comes

Happy ending

But most people did not have enough money to buy one.

The Model T

In the early days, cars were big and they were heavy. They cost a lot to buy. Henry Ford started his own factory.

His Model B cost $2,000.

His Model F cost $1,200.

But Ford thought that the cars of the future should be small and light. They should not cost much to buy.

Mr. Fixit went to work. He built Model K. Make it light. Next came Model N. Keep the cost down. Then came Model R. Make it tough. Next came Model S. Fix the motor. Down the alphabet of models went Mr. Fixit.

Finally came Model T. Build it. Test it.
Tear it apart. Tinker with it. Build it up
again. Test it. Tear it down. Tinker.
Build it up.

At last, Model T was ready.

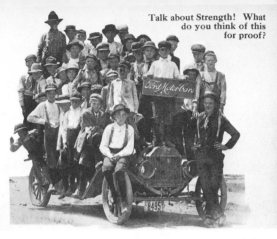

Was it tough!

Was it simple, and was it light!

It could go anywhere!

It could do anything!

The price of the first Model T's was only $850. They began to sell. Ford made a profit.

Ford dropped the price to $600. Still he made a profit.

He dropped the price again. Model T's cost only $360. Still Ford made a profit.

Down went the price to $290. Still Ford made a profit.

The price had dropped and dropped and dropped. Still Ford made a profit. Why?

The first cars were built by hand.
A few people made all the parts for one car.
Then they put the parts together to build
the car. Every person did many jobs. The
workers worked hard. They worked fast. But
building a car still took a lot of time.
So the first cars cost a lot of money.

The way to make cars, said Henry
Ford, was to make them as much alike as
pins. So Ford's workers made many copies of
each part, all exactly the same. The parts
went to one factory where they were all
put together. Each person did a few jobs.
They worked hard. They worked fast.
They made cars faster. The new way
saved time. Ford's cars cost less to build.
The prices began to drop.

That was how Ford made the first
Model T's. Some workers made only
parts. They were specialists. Others
put the parts together. They moved down
a line of cars, putting on the parts. They
were specialists, too.

FORD'S ASSEMBLY LINE

Then Ford had another idea. He decided to take the cars to the workers. A long rope was hooked onto a car axle and wheels. The rope pulled the axle and wheels along. All along the way, people stood still, putting parts on cars. Each worker put on only a few parts. Down the assembly line went the car. The assembly line saved more time. Cars cost still less to build. Ford cut the price of the Model T again.

Then the workers at the Ford factory had an idea of their own. Make the work simpler, they said. They raised the assembly line off the floor. Nobody had to bend over. And each person put on only one part. Some workers put on fenders. Others put on steering wheels. Each person was even more of a specialist.

The new way saved more time. Cars cost even less to build. The price of the Model T dropped again. Finally Ford sold the Model T for $290. Still he made a profit.

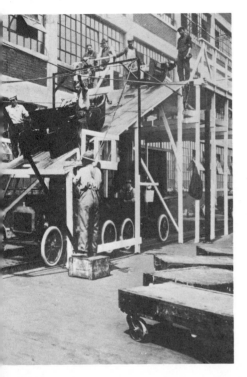

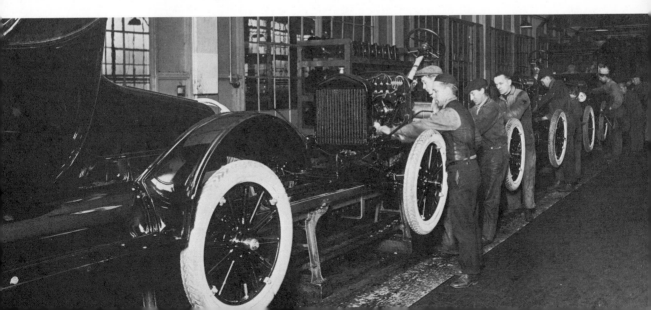

TIN LIZZIE

Ford made Model T's for nineteen years.

They were the first cars
for many families.

Model T's raced from
New York to Seattle.

They could go anywhere.

On any kind of road.

Some people called their Model T's
flivvers. They told each other flivver
stories.

No need for a speedometer on a flivver:

When you go 10 miles an hour, the lamps rattle.

When you go 20 miles an hour, the fenders rattle.

When you go 30 miles an hour, the windshield rattles.

When you go faster than that, your bones rattle.

Some people called their Model T's
Tin Lizzies. They told each other Tin
Lizzie stories.

Question: Why is the Tin Lizzie called a
family car?

Answer: Because it has a muffler for
Dad, a hood for Mother, and
lots of rattles for the kids to
play with.

Ford built 15 million Model T's.
Almost as many stories were told about
the car that could go anywhere and do
anything.

Cars Changed the City

Tin Lizzies and other cars were sold all over the land. Cars were everywhere. They went into town, out of town, uptown, downtown, across town, and around town.

When cars began to chug, cities began to change.

New roads were built. Dirt roads and plank roads were paved. More sidewalks were put in. Highways went from city to city. Service stations were built. Parking lots and garages opened for business. All over the United States, cities were changing.

One city that changed was St. Louis.

St. Louis today

HOW ST. LOUIS CHANGED

Long ago, when people rode in wagons, St. Louis was a small city. Winding trails and roads went in and out of town. When St. Louis was a wagon city, the trails and roads looked like long pieces of string on the map.

Wagon City

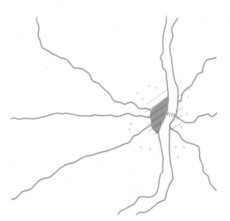

Then came the railroads. St. Louis began to change. It began to grow. Houses and stores were built along the tracks, in long lines going out from the city. When St. Louis was a railroad city, the tracks looked like a big star on the map.

Railroad City

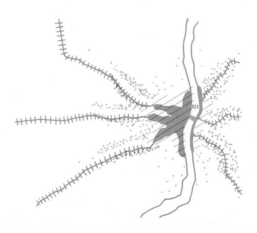

Then came the streetcars. St. Louis began to change again. It grew still larger. Streetcar lines were built all over the city. When St. Louis was a streetcar city, the lines looked like a spider web on the map.

Streetcar City

Then came the cars. St. Louis changed even more. It grew even larger. Cars could go anywhere. St. Louis began to spread out. St. Louis became a car city. A belt was built all around it. The belt was a highway around the city.

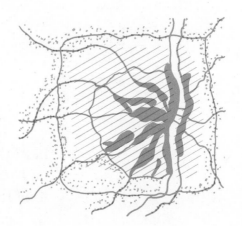

Car City

St. Louis people could live where they wanted. They could drive to work. They could drive to the stores. They could drive to see their friends. They could drive almost any place they wanted to go.

Today, nearly everybody lives in a car city. Not everyone owns a car. But there are many, many cars in the city. Cars changed every city all over the land.

SPACE FOR PARKING

Cars need space to stop and park in the city. Space for parking is a big problem, especially in the C.B.D. In some cities, most of the space is used for streets and parking.

People park their cars on the streets, in parking lots, and in big garages. Parking places for cars use the space of a city. Sometimes underground space is used for parking garages.

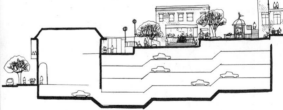

Even dead cars use the space of a city.

Piggly Wiggly was one of the first stores to build parking lots for people in cars. People shopped at Piggly Wiggly because parking was easy. Inside the Piggly Wiggly store were rows and rows of food. The shoppers pushed carts up and down the rows and picked out the food they needed. Shopping at Piggly Wiggly was almost like working on an assembly line.

Other food stores built parking lots for people in cars. Today these stores are called supermarkets. It all started with cars and finding space for parking. It all started with stores like Piggly Wiggly.

But why should every store build its
own parking lot? Why not put many stores
in the same place so they could all build
one parking lot? Many stores together
around one parking lot is called a
shopping center.

One of the first shopping centers was
Country Club Plaza, in Kansas City, Kansas.

Today shopping centers are being
built in the suburbs of many cities. One of
the largest and newest is Roosevelt Field
Shopping Center, in Garden City, New York.

Piggly Wiggly, the supermarket, and
the shopping center have changed the city.
It all started with cars like Tin Lizzie and
finding space for parking.

SPACE FOR MOVING

Moving cars need space in the city.

They need space for turning.

They need space to go fast.

They need space to move slowly.

Highways use space to speed cars in, out, and around the city. Some highways go around the central city. Some push into the central city.

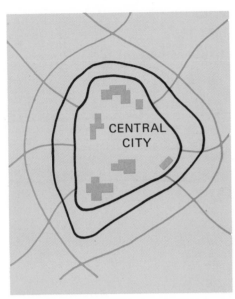

Highways around the central city

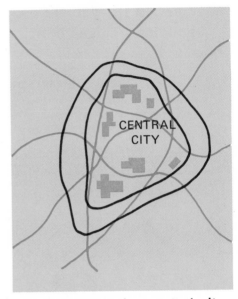

Highways into the central city

Some highways use air space in the city. These highways are called skyways. Cars can cross under them easily. But they cost a lot to build. And they spoil the view.

Some highways use ground space. They are built flat on the ground. These highways are cheaper to build. But often they are hard to cross. They can spoil the beauty of a city, too.

Some highways are sunk into the ground. They are easy to cross. They cost more to build, but they soften the noise of the traffic. Most of the sunken highways also spoil the beauty of a city.

City highways of the future might be different. They might use space inside buildings. This is how they might look.

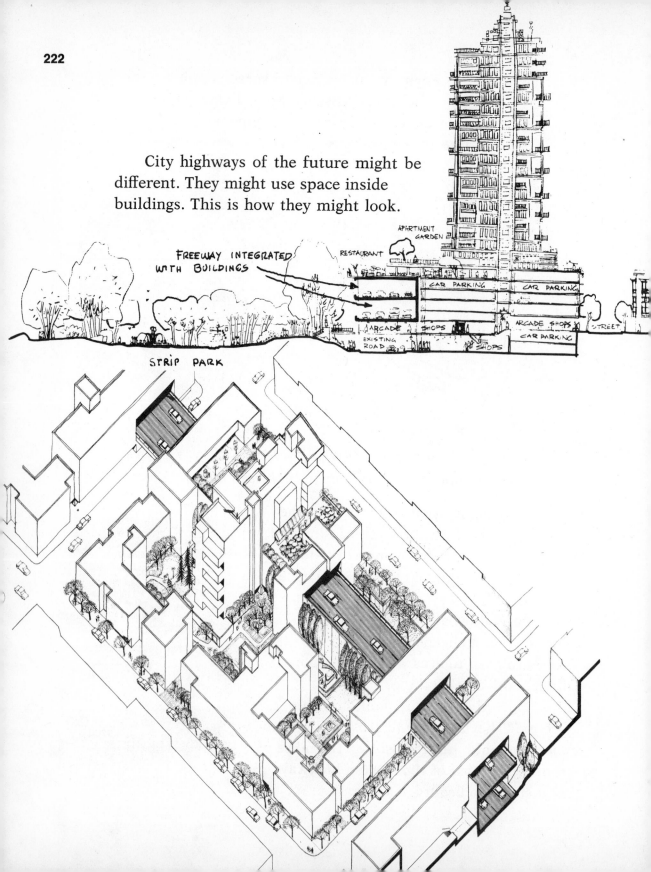

FREEWAY INTEGRATED WITH BUILDINGS

RESTAURANT

APARTMENT GARDEN

CAR PARKING

CAR PARKING

ARCADE SHOPS

ARCADE SHOPS

STREET

EXISTING ROAD

SHOPS

CAR PARKING

STRIP PARK

7

River and Cloud

Water

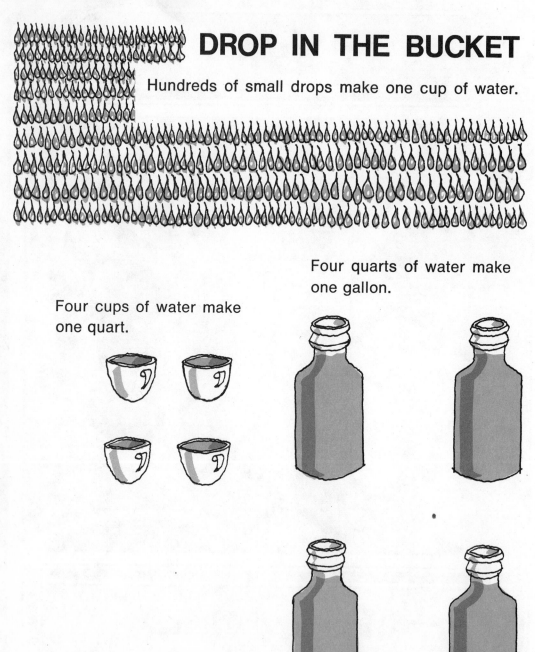

DROP IN THE BUCKET

Hundreds of small drops make one cup of water.

Four quarts of water make one gallon.

Four cups of water make one quart.

Sixty gallons is about enough
water for one person for one day.
Sixty gallons of water will fill
two bathtubs to the top and
spill over into a third bathtub.

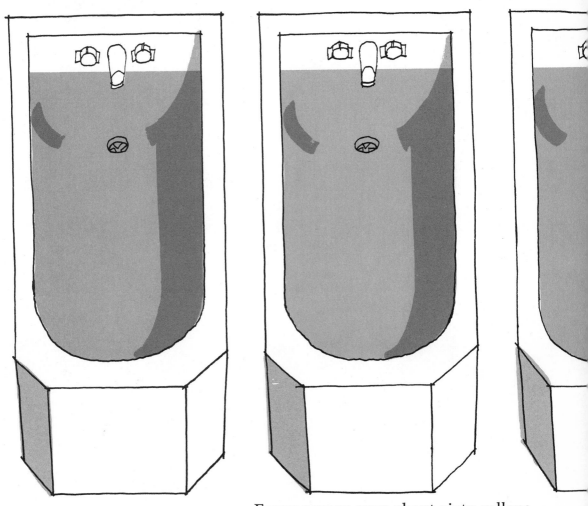

Every person uses about sixty gallons
of water every day. This is the water
you use for drinking, washing, and
cooking.

But the sixty gallons of water you use
is only a drop in the bucket.

Gallons and Gallons

Do you know how much water it takes to run a washing machine one time? Do you know how much water it takes to grow wheat for one loaf of bread? Do you know how much water is needed to make steel for one car? Do you know how much water is used to make one ton of rubber for tires?

Well, it is more than a drop in the bucket.

It takes 30 gallons of water to run a washing machine one time.

It takes 300 gallons of water to grow wheat for one loaf of bread.

It takes 40 thousand gallons of water to make steel for one car.

It takes 660 thousand gallons of water to make one ton of rubber for tires.

CITY WATER

Where does all the water come from? How does your sixty gallons get to you? How does the water get to the wheat field and the steel mill and the rubber tire factory? How do cities get all the water they need for people and factories?

Cities do three things to get water to where it is needed. They find the water and store it. They move the water and make it pure. They get rid of the water after it is used.

Finding and Storing Water

Most big cities go miles and miles into their hinterlands to find water. Some cities, like Chicago, pump water from deep wells. But most city water comes from far-off lakes and rivers.

Cities build dams to store water. They build reservoirs, too.

Some cities store their water in tanks that sit on hills or high in the air on steel towers.

Moving Water and Making It Pure

Turn on a faucet in your home. Out pours the water, safe to drink. Do you know where the water comes from? Do you know why it is safe to drink?

Pipes in the wall behind the faucet go down to the water meter. The meter shows how much water you use.

Pipes from the water meter go under the ground to the street. Under the street runs a water main. The water main goes to the city water works.

Behind the water works is another large pipe. It runs to a dam or reservoir or water tank.

Pumps move the water through the pipes. Chemicals make it clean.

Getting Rid of Water

When you pour water in the sink, it goes down the drain. When you take a shower, the soapy water goes down the drain. Where does the drain water go?

Pipes under the drain take the water out to the sewer under the street. Pipes from the sewer run down to the city sewage plant. The sewage water is made clean in the plant. The clean water goes into a stream or a river. From there, it goes down to the sea, or into a large lake.

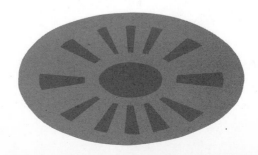

Down the Drain

CAN A LAKE DIE?

LAKE ERIE
Connecticut River

The water people use goes down the drain. The water factories use goes down the drain, too. What happens to all the water and waste from factories?

Parents remember that when they were young, they could swim and fish in Lake Erie. But then the lake became poisoned.

Lake Erie is on the border between Canada and the United States. Look at the map. Can you find all the cities and places that dump waste into Lake Erie?

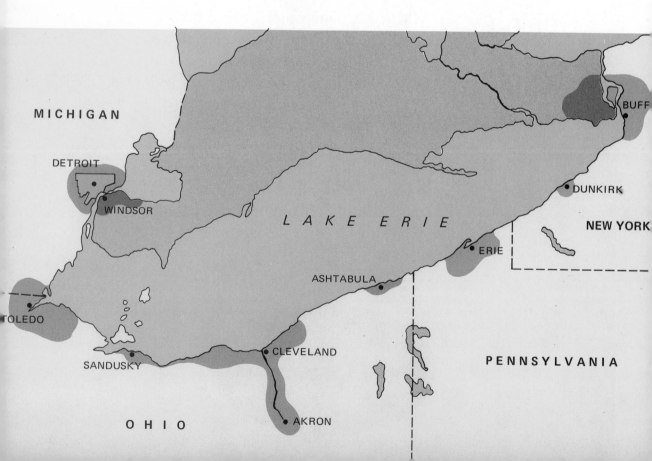

MICHIGAN

DETROIT

WINDSOR

LAKE ERIE

BUFF

DUNKIRK

NEW YORK

ERIE

ASHTABULA

TOLEDO

CLEVELAND

PENNSYLVANIA

SANDUSKY

OHIO

AKRON

Lake Erie is the most polluted of the five Great Lakes. Factories along the banks seem to bleed into it. In some parts of Lake Erie, there are large pools of red and yellow water. This water is very warm. It causes algae plants to grow. When the algae grow thick, nothing else can live in the water.

All lakes grow old. They fill up with mud. They fill up with waste from cities and factories. A lake can die if it fills up with too much waste.

Waste from cities and factories changed the water in Lake Erie. Fish that swam in the lake couldn't live there anymore. Ducks that once came to Lake

Erie couldn't live there anymore. Beavers that used to build dams along the banks of the lake weren't there anymore, either.

But then the fish, ducks, and beavers started coming back to Lake Erie. Cities and factories were dumping less waste in the lake. Lake Erie is still polluted but it is becoming cleaner.

CAN A RIVER DIE?

Sweet Water

The Connecticut River was once one of the most beautiful rivers in the world. People used to say that when the salmon swam upstream, a person could put on snowshoes and walk across the river on their backs.

Old-timers in the Connecticut Valley had a special word for the clear, cold water of the river. The water tasted so good they called it sweet. Up and down the valley, the water of the Connecticut River was sweet.

Then the salmon left the river. Tires and tin cans took their place. What happened to the beautiful Connecticut? What happened to the sweet water?

The Muck Closed In

During a summer not long ago, twenty boys and their teacher set out in canoes. They canoed all the way down the long Connecticut River.

At first, they drank from the river. "Then the muck closed in," said Mike.

"Sometimes we wanted to quit because it was so ugly," said Dunne.

Ten of the boys became sick one afternoon when the group paddled through dead fish and sewage.

One day, they saw a beer can dump. Thousands of cans were falling into the river.

The boys counted twenty-three town dumps at the edge of the river. Three boys counted sewers. They gave up on the second day. There were too many to count.

Near a steam plant in one city, they could feel the heat of the water through the bottoms of their boats.

They had to paddle around wrecked cars dumped into the river.

One boy thought, "It's like killing the United States to make that valley ugly."

Can a river die?

CAN A RIVER COME BACK TO LIFE?

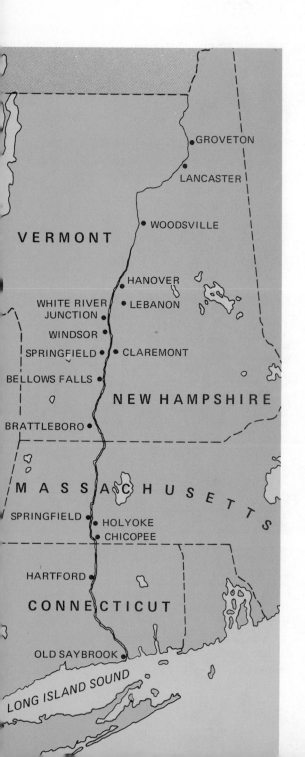

The Connecticut River water is used over and over. Cities and factories up the river use water and dump it back again. Down the river goes the used water. Cities and factories down the river use the water again. They dump it back into the river. Down it goes. A drop of water used in Holyoke, Massachusetts, might be used two times or more before it gets to Long Island Sound.

Some cities and factories dump warm water and waste into the river. Algae grow very fast. More and more algae soon kill the other river plants. Fish and birds and other animals can't live in algae water. The algae show that the river is polluted.

Team Work

The Connecticut River is used by cities and factories in four states. All the states are working together to save the river. The states formed a team and gave it a name almost as long as the river itself. It is called the New England Interstate Water Pollution Control Commission. But, for short, it is known as the C. C.

The C. C. watches the river and reports on the pollution. The C. C. also helps factories and cities find better ways to purify water.

The Connecticut River is clear in many places now. Some of the salmon are coming back. If all the cities and all the factories purify their water, it will be a beautiful river once more. Someday, the water will be sweet again.

Air

DIVE IN!

You live at the bottom of an ocean of air.
You have lived there all your life. Dive in!
Look around. Listen. Swallow a breath
of air from the ocean around you.

What to See

Look for the fog that hugs the ground. See the lightning scratch the sky. Follow a floating snowflake. Watch a line of clouds march across the sky. Find your rainbow in the wide ocean of air.

What to Hear

Listen to the small sound of the breeze in the trees. Listen to the big sound when the wind fills your ears. Listen to the rattle of hail on the roof. Hear the thunder roll around the ocean of air.

What to Swallow

Do not swallow drifting smoke in the ocean of air. Do not swallow gas and dust at the bottom of the air ocean. But do swallow a breath of air on a clear morning. Catch a snowflake on your tongue. Swallow the air in a long, sleepy yawn.

CLEANING THE AIR OCEAN

Down in the ocean of air are the cities people live in. You must help to keep the air clean in the cities. You must help to keep your air ocean clean.

Nature is always cleaning the air ocean around you. Wind cleans the air. Rain cleans the air.

Mixing

When winds blow, they mix clean air from some places with dirty air from other places. So the dirty air gets a little cleaner. And the clean air gets a little dirtier. But that is like cleaning your room by putting your toys all over the house. Your room is cleaner, but the whole house is dirtier.

Sinking

Dust sinks through the air ocean to the ground. It falls on trees and houses and cars. The trees get dusty. So do the houses and the cars. But the air gets cleaner.

Washing

The best cleaner of all is rain. Rain cleans the air ocean. It washes out the dust, smoke, and gas. After a rainstorm, the sky is blue. It's good to be at the bottom of the ocean of air.

The Tulsa Mystery

Scientists are like detectives. Both solve mysteries. A detective solves crime mysteries. A scientist solves mysteries about the world.

The rainfall in the city of Tulsa is a scientific mystery. There are some very surprising facts about the rainfall in Tulsa, Oklahoma.

How to Measure Rainfall

Find a big bottle with straight up and down sides. Hold a ruler next to the bottle. With a crayon, mark off the inches. Put a funnel in the top of the bottle. Take the bottle outside. After it rains, see how many inches of rain fell into your rain bottle.

Weather stations have metal tubes to measure the rainfall. Weather forecasters use special sticks to see how many inches of rain fell in one day.

FACTS ABOUT TULSA
Rainfall in Tulsa

The bar graph shows what some weather forecasters found out about the rainfall in Tulsa. It shows years and inches of rain.

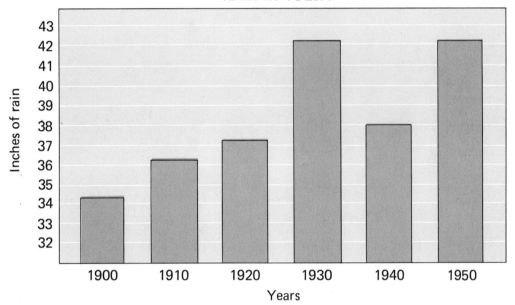

RAIN IN TULSA

What happened to the rainfall in Tulsa? Did it rain less and less? Did it rain more and more? Why do you think this happened?

Population in Tulsa

This bar graph shows how Tulsa grew. The population of Tulsa grew bigger and bigger.

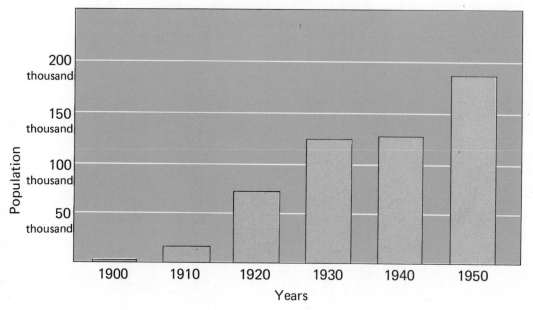

POPULATION IN TULSA

Do you think population had anything to do with more rain in Tulsa? Do you think numbers of people and inches of rain have anything to do with each other?

A Careful Guess

Why did Tulsa get more and more rain?

The population of Tulsa grew and grew. Could more people make it rain more? Is this a real mystery?

What are the facts about rainfall and population in Tulsa, Oklahoma?

1. More and more rain fell.
2. The population grew bigger and bigger.

It looks like these two facts go together. It looks like more people means more rain. You can put facts together and make a careful guess. Here is a careful guess about the rain and population facts for Tulsa:

Tulsa seemed to get more and more rain as its population became bigger and bigger.

CLUES TO THE MYSTERY

Scientists often write down what they
think or find out. They also read what
other scientists write. Reading what
other scientists write is one way to find
clues to a mystery.

Dr. H. E. Landsberg has studied
the weather of cities. He wrote about this.
His report was printed in a book called
*Man's Role in Changing the Face of the
Earth*. Here are some of Dr. Landsberg's
ideas about the weather in cities and
why it changes. What clues can you find
about the Tulsa mystery?

Wind

A city has many buildings. Some are very tall. Glass, stone, brick, and steel are used to make them.

City buildings are tall and hard. They hold back the wind. They change the way the wind moves. When the wind changes, the weather changes. Buildings change the weather of a city.

Heat

Every person in a city adds heat to the air ocean. Car motors add heat. Stoves and furnaces heat buildings. Some of the heat escapes from the buildings. It warms the air.

The sun warms glass, stone, brick, and steel. They give off heat, too. The air gets hotter. Even air conditioners and refrigerators add heat to the city air.

A city has many people, cars, stoves, furnaces, and buildings. They all add heat to the air. They all change the weather of a city.

Dust

Every city is like a car engine. When a car engine works, it adds smoke, dust, and gases to the air. When a city works, it adds smoke, dust, and gases to the air. Smoke, dust, and gases change the weather of a city.

The La Porte Mystery

Cities are made by people. The cities people build may change the weather. This mystery is about a change in the weather in La Porte. La Porte is a city in Indiana.

Find La Porte on the map. Find South Bend. It is about twenty miles from La Porte. Find Valparaiso. It is also about twenty miles from La Porte.

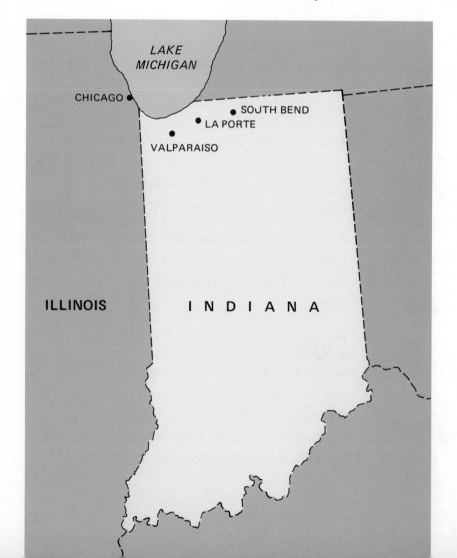

IS THE MYSTERY REAL?

Here are facts about rainfall in 1960
for South Bend, La Porte, and Valparaiso.
One town got much more rain.

RAINFALL, 1960

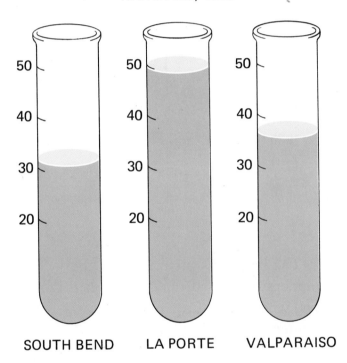

SOUTH BEND   LA PORTE   VALPARAISO

La Porte got much more rain than
the other two towns. Why should La Porte
get more rain? Can you make a guess?

La Porte's heavy rainfall was first
noticed by Mr. Stanley Changnon. Mr.
Changnon asked himself, "Is the mystery
real?"

Let's See

Does La Porte really get more rain? Maybe 1960 was just a funny year for rain. What happened in 1950? What happened in 1940? Look for yourself.

RAINFALL FOR THREE CITIES

YEAR	CITY		
	South Bend	La Porte	Valparaiso
1960	32 inches	50 inches	38 inches
1950	36	53	37
1940	33	48	37
1930	38	43	40
1920	30	34	34
1910	38	37	—

The scientists also checked the thunderstorm record. They looked for days when only La Porte had thunderstorms. They called these Solo Thunderstorm Days. Between 1951 and 1964, La Porte had almost 200 Solo Thunderstorm Days.

Then the scientists looked at the records for hail days. They found that between 1951 and 1965, La Porte had 128 hail days. South Bend had only 30.

What do you think? Is the mystery real?

A SCIENTIFIC ANSWER

There is a scientific way to solve the La Porte mystery.

This graph has a big bump. The big bump shows when La Porte had many rainy days. When did the big bump happen?

Two Big Bumps

RAIN IN LA PORTE

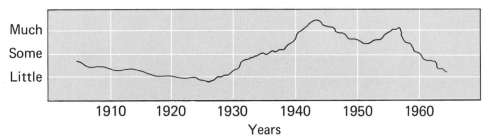

Here is a graph about Chicago. It also has a big bump. The big bump shows when Chicago had many smoke and haze days. Haze is another name for very fine dust in the air. When did the big bump happen?

SMOKE AND HAZE DAYS IN CHICAGO

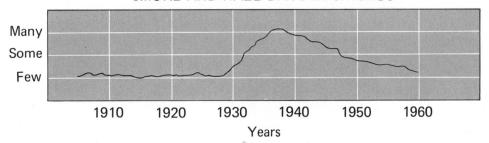

Each graph has a big bump at about the same time. La Porte got more and more rain when Chicago got more and more smoke and haze.

Factories and Wind

How could smoke and haze in Chicago make it rain more in La Porte? Look at the map. Where is Chicago? Is it near La Porte?

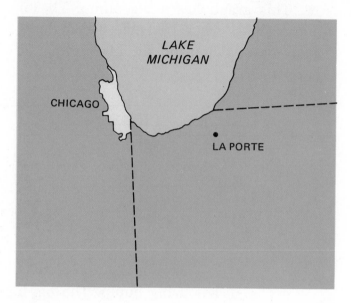

Chicago is a very big city. It has many people, cars, stoves, furnaces, and buildings. It has many factories, too. Factories add lots of smoke, heat, dust, gases, and steam to the air.

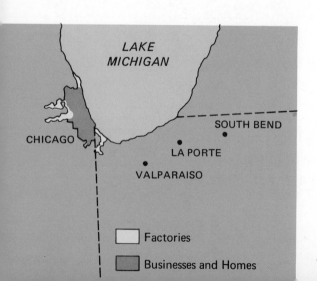

This map shows where the houses and businesses are in Chicago. It shows where the factories are around Chicago.

This picture shows the air above the factories in Chicago.

The smoke, heat, dust, gases, and steam from the factories help to form rain clouds. But La Porte is many miles away from Chicago. How do the rain clouds get to La Porte? Can you tell from this map?

HOW THE WIND BLOWS

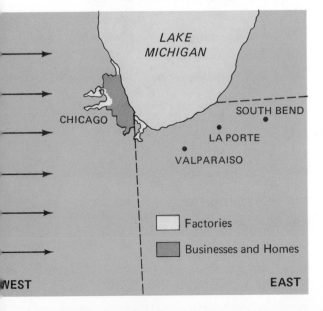

Why does La Porte get more rain than South Bend and Valparaiso? Can you use the graphs and maps to find the answer?

Trapped

SMOGIGATED

Air over cities is often trapped. Here is what happens in Los Angeles when air over the city is trapped.

Los Angeles sometimes looks like this from an airplane. The brown cloud is smog. Los Angeles has smoggy days more than half the year. The smog makes people's eyes water. It makes it hard for them to breathe.

When the smog is very thick, children playing outside sometimes say they have been "smogigated."

Upside-Down Air

Smog in Los Angeles looks like this from the ground. Do you see the blue sky up high and the smog down low? Why does the smog lie low over the city?

Air is usually warmest close to the ground. When air gets warm, it rises. As it goes higher, it cools.

This graph shows the air up high and down low over Los Angeles. It shows where the air is warm and where it is cool.

Up High	Cool	Cool	Cool	Cool	Warm	Warm	Warm	Warm	Warm	Warm	Warm	Cool
Down Low	Warm	Warm	Warm	Warm	Cool	Cool	Cool	Cool	Cool	Cool	Cool	Warm
	JAN.	FEB.	MAR.	APR.	MAY	JUNE	JULY	AUG.	SEPT.	OCT.	NOV.	DEC.

That's a surprise! From May to the end of November, the higher up you go over Los Angeles, the warmer the air gets.

For seven months, the air is turned upside down. When the cool air near the ground gets warm, it starts to rise. It rises over Los Angeles until it reaches the layer of warm air. Then it stops. The city air is trapped. Dust is trapped. Smoke is trapped. The sun cooks the trapped air until it turns brown.

WHO DID IT?

The Slow Killer

At first, it was just the needles. They turned yellow. They could not make food for the tree. Time passed. The yellow needles dropped off. Then there was even less food for life.

More time passed. New needles grew back. But they were short. Short needles made only a little food.

Time passed. Roots died. Still less food.

Still more time passed. Branches dropped off. Even less food.

Beetles began to attack.

In five years, the pine tree was dead.

What Killed the People Trees?

Lake Arrowhead is in the mountains about fifty miles from Los Angeles. But winds blow from the Pacific Ocean over the city and toward the mountains. They blow the smog from Los Angeles into the pine forest at Lake Arrowhead.

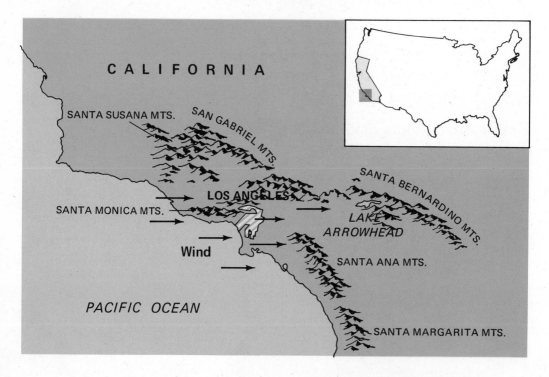

CALIFORNIA

SANTA SUSANA MTS.
SAN GABRIEL MTS.
SANTA BERNARDINO MTS.
LOS ANGELES
SANTA MONICA MTS.
LAKE ARROWHEAD
SANTA ANA MTS.
Wind
PACIFIC OCEAN
SANTA MARGARITA MTS.

Smog is slowly killing a million pine trees at Lake Arrowhead. Some of the dying trees are more than a hundred years old. Many trees have already been cut down and sold for lumber.

New trees are being planted. But the old trees will be missed. People camped under them. They picnicked and hiked under them, too. They were people trees.

What Can Be Done?

Smog is caused by trapped air. So far, scientists do not know how to break the trap. They do not know how to stop the sun from cooking the smog. They do not know how to stop the wind from blowing the smog to Lake Arrowhead. What can be done?

The scientists do know that most smog comes from car engines. A car engine sends smoke, dust, and gases into the air. The scientists and the cities must find ways to stop these and make the air cleaner.

If people used their cars less, the air would be cleaner. More fast trains and subways will help people use their cars less. Some cities are building fast trains. Some cities have subways so people can ride without their cars.

If car engines were changed, the air would be cleaner. Some scientists have invented new electric engines and steam engines for cars.

Other scientists are changing the gasoline that cars use. Still others are changing the engines themselves.

New trains, more subways, new engines, and new gasoline all cost extra money. Will the cost be worth it? How much are the people trees worth?

How to Mine a City

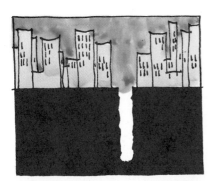

Years ago, people would say, "There's gold in them thar hills!" They would start looking for a gold vein in the rock under the earth. When they found a vein, they dug a deep hole called a shaft. They brought the rock up out of the shaft. They crushed the rock and took out the gold. They called this mining the earth for gold.

There's a man in the city who has a mine.
He found a vein right in front of his house.
His vein is the leaves in the street.

He rakes leaves on the sidewalk.

He rakes leaves in the gutter.

He rakes up every leaf he can find and
takes it to a big pile in his backyard.

All winter, the pile sits. The pile gets hot.
It grows smaller. It grows even smaller.
In the spring, all that is left is a small pile of
compost. Compost is rich in food for
the soil.

In the springtime, he uses a machine to
spread the compost on his lawn. The lawn
grows rich, green, and thick.

MINES IN THE CITY

A city can be a mine. Look around
your city. See if you can find a vein
to mine.

Here's one.

Here's one, too.

Here is a rich vein.

Have you discovered how your city is
like a mine? Have you found out how
to mine your city?

THE HISTORY OF THIS PAGE

Hey! Look down here. Right under your nose. Page 266, that's me, T. Page! Read my print and I'll tell you the history of me—This Page.

China and Mexico

My pop's family came from China a long time ago. They were made of mulberry bark.

My mom's family got their start in Mexico with the Mayan Indians. It could have been in Tikal. Anyway, Mayan paper was made from the soft bark of the fig tree. But almost every Mayan book was burned by the Spanish. So, little is known about Mayan paper.

Timbuktu and England

My cousins may have been pages in the books at Timbuktu. The Moslems learned to make paper from the Chinese. Later, the Moslems taught the Spanish how to make paper. Finally, in 1494, paper making reached England. By then, Columbus had sailed to America.

A Seedling

I started as a tree seedling. I
just stood there. The sun shone.
Rain fell. And I grew as fast
as I knew how.

One day, a logger cut me down.
Off I went to the mill. They
cut me into short pieces. They
took off my bark. Did I ever
look funny!

Chips and Pulp

Next I went to the chipper.
Boy, did that tickle!

Then they dumped me into the
digester. That was soggy!
By that time, I was wood pulp.

Pressed and Dried

They dumped me into a tank of water and turned on the beaters. On I went to be pressed into a sheet. Then I was dried and put on a reel.

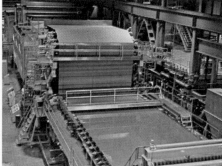

Printed and Bound

Next they cut me into sheet. The printer put these black letters all over my new white suit. The binder put me into this book.

So here I am.
I'm down here, and you're up there.
Say, what's your history?

BICYCLE, TRICYCLE, RECYCLE

A bicycle has two wheels. That's why it is called a bi-cycle. "Bi" means two. A tricycle has three wheels. That is why it is called tri-cycle. "Tri" means three. "Cycle" means to go around in a circle.

Cycle

Many things go around in a cycle. The dishes in your house go around in a cycle.

Recycle

Each time you sit down to eat, the dishes go around the cycle again. They are re-cycled. "Re" means again. You use your dishes over and over again.

Paper

Every year, a family of four people use about 2,000 pounds of paper. That's a whole ton. They throw the paper away and use new paper each year.

Paper is made of wood pulp. Wood pulp can come from trees. It takes 17 trees to make enough wood pulp for 2,000 pounds of paper.

Wood pulp can also come from inside the city. Old paper can be used to make wood pulp. The city can be a concrete forest.

Paper is all over the city. Boxes, books, letters, newspapers, posters all use paper. You can collect these. You can take all the paper to the paper mill. The mill can use the old paper instead of trees to make wood pulp. You can recycle paper.

You can also recycle metal and glass. You can recycle water and air. The city can be a mine. You can mine the city.

Mining the City

City Planning

People and Their Cities

Most people do not study cities very much. They just live in them. They do not think much about city problems and how to fix them.

Most people love their cities. They love them even though cities are crowded and the noise gets worse every day. Oh, they complain about the trash and the smog. But they love their cities anyway.

They hardly notice that their cities grow and grow. They do not often see the problems that are getting worse. They go to the spots they like. They stay away from the spots they don't like. The city they see is just fine.

"Anyway, the smog here is not as bad as the smog there," you can hear someone say.

"That city has even worse slums than our city," someone else will say.

A CLOSER LOOK

City planners take a closer look at cities and their problems. They do not look at just the parts they like in the city.

City planners study cities and how they grow. They try to find out why some cities grow fast and why others grow slowly. They see the ugly and dangerous spots in cities. They see the beautiful and interesting places.

City planners work in two ways.

Some city planners start from scratch. They plan new cities. They want the new cities to have everything people will need. They also want the new cities to look beautiful.

The other city planners study cities that were built long ago and just grew. They tear down parts of these old cities. They build new houses, offices, and parks in the old spaces.

Both kinds of city planners work for the future. They hope that every corner of every city will be a good place for people to live in. They want cities to be lively and interesting for grown-ups. They want cities to be healthy and fun for children.

Boston

Old Planned Cities

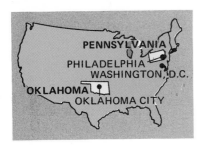

Cities sit where they do for reasons. People choose places to build cities for good reasons. But today you cannot always find out the reasons why old cities sit where they do.

Sometimes you cannot see why old cities were built where they were. And sometimes you cannot see why they grew the way they did. Some cities grew in a hit-or-miss way.

But many old cities were planned. Sometimes the city plans were good. Sometimes the plans were bad. Sometimes even the best plans did not turn out the way the planners wanted.

BUILT IN A HUNDRED DAYS

Oklahoma City is often called "The City Built in a Hundred Days."

A day in 1889 was set for the beginning of Oklahoma City. On that day, the United States government was giving away land in Oklahoma to settlers. The land was free. Only the land that belonged to the Indian tribes could not be taken.

Rush for Land

A man called Mr. Wicks went to Oklahoma City on that day. Later, he wrote the story of what happened.

Thousands of people lined up at the Oklahoma border, ready for the wild rush for land. Mr. Wicks was among them. At noon, cannons boomed. Shots rang out. The people rushed for land. Many ran for Oklahoma City.

In Oklahoma City, the land was marked out in lots. Everyone raced around looking for a good lot, Mr. Wicks said. The people were all mixed up, and they acted like stray sheep.

The race was over, Mr. Wicks wrote, when a family found a lot they liked. They hurried to drive in their stakes. They rushed to put up their tents. They had to "improve" their land before night came or someone could "jump" their claim. To "jump" a claim means to steal the land somebody has found.

Unjumpable

Mr. Wicks found a corner lot. He drove in his stakes. Then he threw blankets over his cot and staked them to the ground. Mr. Wicks had "improved" his land, and, he said, his claim was "unjumpable."

That night, Mr. Wicks had trouble sleeping because of the shouting. But, by morning, everyone was fine. The settlers worked hard. Tents came down. Cabins went up.

What Kind of Life?

Would you like to live in a city that was built in a hundred days? The lots were all planned out. But what was missing? What would life be like in such a city?

Oklahoma City was a planned city. Was it a good plan?

UNDER PENN'S HAT

In the center of Philadelphia stands a statue of William Penn in his Quaker hat. Pigeons sit on the hat. Its turned-up brim holds the rain. Birds drink the soft rainwater.

Many people look around Philadelphia and shake their heads sadly. They are sad because of what is happening "under Penn's hat."

City of Brotherly Love

The king of England gave Pennsylvania to young William Penn. Penn planned a city near one end of his large piece of land. He wanted a place where the Quakers could live together in peace.

Penn called his city "Philadelphia." This means "city of brotherly love." Philadelphia was built where the Delaware River meets the Schuylkill River.

William Penn planned his city with green square parks at four corners. His plan looked like this.

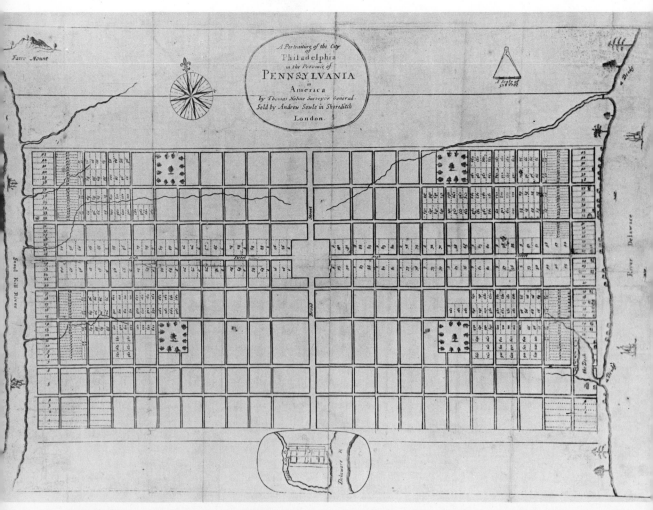

Can you see the parks William Penn planned three hundred years ago? The city of Philadelphia grew around the parks.

Philadelphia was a beautiful city. Ships sailed in and out of its bright, clean harbor. Ships were built there, too. Families lived in neat rows of brick houses with marble steps.

Some More Planning

Philadelphia grew and grew. It filled up with many people. Later, there was smog. The clean, bright harbor was not clean and bright anymore. The brick houses with marble steps had been built for one family each. But then three or four or even ten families lived in each one. Many streets became slums.

The people of Philadelphia remember William Penn's plans for a beautiful city. City planners are planning parts of the city over again. They think Philadelphia can be beautiful once more.

THE NATION'S CAPITAL

President George Washington rode out on his horse to look at land along the Potomac River. The new nation was going to build a special capital city. And President Washington wanted to pick a good place.

Each day, from the middle of October until the end of October, he rode up and down beside the Potomac River looking at the land. But it is hard to choose the place to put a nation's capital. George Washington talked with Thomas Jefferson about the problem. He talked with many congressmen, too. At last, a spot was chosen. Washington, D.C., was soon being planned.

A Very Special City

Washington, D.C., was planned as a very special city.

In the first place, it was the biggest city that had ever been planned for the United States.

In the second place, it was an exciting end to a dream—that this nation should rule itself.

In the third place, it was the start of a new dream—that the United States would become a rich, happy nation.

In the fourth place, leaders like Washington and Jefferson helped to plan the city.

In the fifth place, it was planned by a famous city planner who came from France. When Washington, D.C., was finally built, it stood as a model for other cities. Many ideas in it were new. Cities all over the world copied parts of this fine capital city.

Some More Planning

Washington grew up and out. Parts of it
became ugly and crowded. It did not look
like the dream of Washington and Jefferson.
Other planners and builders took up the
work. They are trying to make Washington
as beautiful as its planners had dreamed.

A City Mix

Some city planners used to think that all city blocks should be big. They wanted to have all the houses in one place. They wanted to put all the apartment buildings in another place. They wanted to put the businesses in still another place. They wanted all the stores to be in one place close together.

Other planners did not like this idea. They wanted to build a little bit of everything in each part of the city. They wanted a city mix!

San Francisco

HOW TO MIX A CITY

City planners know that the places people like best in cities never have all of one thing. The spots city people like are gay and noisy. They are short blocks, with many places to live and places to eat and hotels and parks and stores all close together. People go most to places that are colorful and exciting.

City planners watched the people and thought, We'd better plan cities the way people like them. People like a mix of things!

Each block should have big buildings and little buildings, they said. Each block should have old places and new places.

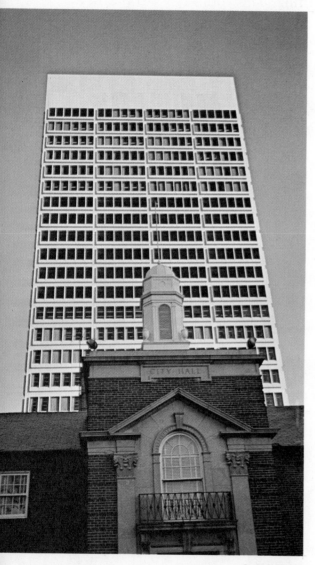

St. Louis

Philadelphia

A street in Los Angeles

Skating in New York's Rockefeller Center

Each block should have many uses. Some people should work there. Some people should play and rest there. Others should live there all the time. A lively spot has a good mix. City people will like to work and live there, and other people will like to visit it.

A Good Example

On Park Avenue in New York City are many tall modern buildings. The fountains spray diamond drops of water into the sun.

But if you were a city planner, you could sit outside these buildings at noon and notice something very odd.

Hundreds of workers come out of the buildings at lunchtime. But most of them do not walk up and down Park Avenue to enjoy the fountains and the fine buildings. As soon as they come to the corner, they turn east toward Lexington Avenue or west toward Madison Avenue.

What does Lexington Avenue have
that Park Avenue does not have?

What magnet draws the people to
Madison Avenue? Why do they spend their
lunch hour walking there instead of
strolling along Park Avenue?

A LITTLE BIT OF EVERYTHING

City planners know that most people like a city mix. People like big modern buildings. But they also like little stores where they can buy exciting things.

People like noise and excitement and color in their cities. They like to move from spot to spot and find surprises. They like to go from quiet open places to noisy crowded places. They like to buy and look and talk and listen. They like old buildings for some reasons, and they like new buildings for other reasons. They like a little bit of everything.

What would you like, if you lived in a city?
What would you plan, if you were a city planner?

Your Children's Cities

Do you hope that your own children will live in wonderful cities? Do you want them to have cities that are healthy to live in and beautiful to look at?

Do you know who will decide what the cities of the future will be like?

Of course you know. You will decide. You will be the planners and the workers and the voters. You will build and pay for and enjoy the cities of the future.

You will do it when you plan a building or help to put it up. You will do it when you vote for people who will carry out good ideas. You will help, one by one and as members of groups, to build fine cities.

Glossary

FULL PRONUNCIATION KEY

The pronunciation of each word is shown just after the word, in this way: **ab bre vi ate** (ə brē′ vē āt). The letters and signs used are pronounced as in the words below. The mark ′ is placed after a syllable with primary or heavy accent, as in the example above. The mark ′ after a syllable shows a secondary or lighter accent, as in **ab bre vi a tion** (ə brē′ vē ā′ shən).

a	hat, cap	k	kind, seek	u	cup, butter
ā	age, face			u̇	full, put
ä	father, far	l	land, coal	ü	rule, move
b	bad, rob	m	me, am		
ch	child, much	n	no, in		
		ng	long, bring		
				v	very, save
d	did, red	o	hot, rock	w	will, woman
		ō	open, go		
e	let, best	ô	order, all	y	young, yet
ē	equal, be	oi	oil, voice		
ėr	term, learn	ou	house, out	z	zero, breeze
				zh	measure, seizure
f	fat, if	p	paper, cup		
g	go, bag	r	run, try	ə represents:	
h	he, how	s	say, yes	a in about	
		sh	she, rush	e in taken	
i	it, pin	t	tell, it	i in April	
ī	ice, five	th	thin, both	o in lemon	
j	jam, enjoy	ᴛʜ	then, smooth	u in circus	

Acropolis (ə krop′ ə lis), usually, the hill citadel of ancient Athens, here a group of walls on Zimbabwe hill (61)

adobe (ə dō′ bē), a building material made of clay and straw, used for houses in ancient Tikal (53)

aguada (ə gwä′ də), the Spanish word for "waterhole" (36)

Ahagger Mountains (ə hāg′ ər), a rocky plateau region in the north central Sahara (86)

Ah Kukum (ä′ kü′ kum), a Mayan name meaning "the feather" (50)

algae (al′ jē), any of a group of simple aquatic plants, such as seaweed (233)

Algiers (al girz′), an important center of trade in northern Africa. Today it is the capital and largest city of Algeria. (93)

Avendano (ä ven dä′ nō), the missionary priest who discovered the ruins of Tikal (56)

bactun (bak′ tün), a Mayan unit of time, equal to 144,000 days (48)

bajo (bä′ hō), the Spanish word for "marsh" (36)

Bangor (bang′ gôr), a city in southern Maine (180)

bay (bā), an inlet or small body of water set off from the main body of water (181)

Bogota (bō gə tä′), the capital of Colombia (192)

Bosnywash (bäz′ nē wäsh), a name given to the megalopolis on the east coast of the United States; made up of the names Boston, New York, and Washington (193)

cacao bean (kə kā′ ō), the seed of a tropical American tree, from which chocolate is made (51)

Cairo (kī′ rō), an ancient city on the Nile River, now the capital of Egypt (84)

Caribbean Sea (kar ə bē′ ən), a part of the Atlantic Ocean; the body of water enclosing the Yucatan Peninsula (35)

central business district, C.B.D. (sen′ tral biz′ ness dis′ trikt), the main business section of a city (135)

chac (chäk), a Mayan rain god (40)

Chan (chan), a Mayan family name (50)

Chel (chel), a Mayan family name (50)

chilan (chi län′), a Mayan priest (52)

Circleville (sėr' kəl vil), a town in southern Ohio, the site of ancient earthworks (27)

Columbus, Christopher (kə lum' bəs, kris' to fər), Italian explorer who discovered America in 1492 (56)

compost (kom' pōst), a mixture of decomposing organic refuse, used as fertilizer (264)

Cuy (kü' ē), a Mayan nickname meaning "the owl" (50)

cubit (kü' bit), an ancient measure of length, the distance from the tip of the middle finger to the elbow, usually 18–20 inches; in Mohenjo-daro, about 20 inches (78)

density (den' sə tē), quantity or number per unit; here, population per unit of area (148)

desert (dez' ərt), an area with few plants or trees and little water (89, 106)

drowned coastline (droůnd kōst līn), formed when land along the shore sinks below sea-level (180)

estuary (es' chü er ē), a place where ocean tide meets river current at a river's wide mouth (105)

flivver (fliv' ėr), a small, cheap car, applied especially to the Model T Ford (213)

ford (fôrd), a spot in a river or stream where the water is shallow and easily crossed on foot or horseback (101)

Gao (gä' ō), a city in western Africa, part of the ancient Mali Empire (87)

geographer (jē og' rə fər), a person who studies the earth and its life and the relationship between the two (97)

glacier (glā' shėr), a large, slowly moving mass of snow and ice (180)

glyph (glif), a carved figure or symbol (46)

gorge (gôrj), a narrow valley that is much deeper than it is wide (71)

haji (häj' ē), a Moslem who has made a pilgrimage to Mecca (87)

hajj (häj), the pilgrimage to Mecca that every Moslem is supposed to make at least once (87)

Himalayas (him ə lā' əz), a mountain range in northern India; the range in which Mt. Everest is located (70)

hinterlands (hin' tėr landz), the rural areas surrounding the suburbs of a city (168)

Indus (in' dəs), a river which rises in the Himalayas and flows into the Arabian Sea; Mohenjo-daro is located on the Indus (71)

Islam (is′ ləm), the Moslem religion, founded by Mohammed (87)

jaguar (jag′ wär), one of the most vicious cats found in the Americas. The ancient Maya considered the jaguar a god. (40)

Jenne (jen′ ə), a city in western Africa, part of the ancient Mali Empire (87)

katun (ka′ tün), a Mayan unit of time, equal to 7,200 days (48)

kin (kin), a Mayan unit of time, equal to one day (48)

La Porte (lə·pôrt′), a city in northwestern Indiana (250)

Limpopo (lim pō′ pō), a river in southern Africa, which flows through Rhodesia to the Indian Ocean (58)

maize (māz), corn (37)

Mali (mä′ lē), an ancient empire in western Africa (86)

Mambo (mäm′ bō), the ancient Rozwi name for their king (65)

Mandingo (man ding′ gō), a people of western Africa (86)

Mansa Musa (man′ sə mü′ sə), the most powerful ruler of the ancient Mali Empire; reigned 1307–1332 (85)

marsh (märsh), low-lying, wet ground that usually floods in winter and remains wet throughout the year (36)

Maya (mī′ yə), a people of southeastern Mexico and Central America (37)

Mecca (mek′ ə), an Arabian city, the birthplace of Mohammed and holy city of Islam (87)

megalopolis (meg ə lop′ ə lis), an area made up of a group of large cities and their surrounding areas; a "supercity" (193)

milpa (mil′ pə), a term for a small cornfield, used in Mexico since ancient times (37)

Mohammed (mō ham′ id), the founder and prophet of Islam (91)

Mohenjo-daro (mō hen′ jo·da′ rō), the site of an ancient settlement on the Indus River in Pakistan (70)

Monomatapa (mon ō mə tap′ ə), a term for the king who ruled the Zimbabwe area before the coming of the Rozwi (65)

mosque (mosk), a Moslem temple (87)

Mwari (mwar′ e), a god of the Rozwi people (68)

Ngoni (ngō′ nē), an African people who drove the Rozwi from Zimbabwe (66)

Niani (nī än′ ē), a city in western Africa, part of the ancient Mali Empire (87)

Niger (nī′ jėr), a river in western Africa (87)

Oahu (ō ä′ hü), the most populous of the Hawaiian Islands, site of Honolulu (188)

oasis (ō ā′ sis), a watering place in a desert (89)

peninsula (pə nin′ sə la), an area of land surrounded by water on three sides (35)

Piedmont (pēd′ mont), a plateau in the southeastern United States between the Appalachians and the Atlantic coast (182)

plains (plāns), a broad, nearly level area of land that has no sudden change in elevation (91)

plateau (pla tō′), an area of flat, elevated land (91)

Platte (plat), a river on the Great Plains of the United States (110)

Potomac (pə tō′ mək), a river on the east coast of the United States; Washington, D.C. is located on the Potomac (283)

prairie (prəi′ rē), a wide area of level, treeless grassland (106)

rain forest (rān for əst), a densely wooded area in the tropics having a yearly rainfall of at least 100 inches (36)

recycle (rē sī′ kəl), to re-process and use again (269)

reservoir (rez′ ėr vwär), a natural or artificial water storage lake (229)

Rozwi (roz′ wē), an ancient African people, probably the principal builders of Zimbabwe (65)

Sahara (sə hä′ rə), a north African desert; the word itself is Arabic for "desert" (89)

Sanlosdiego (san lōs dē ā′ gō), a name given to the megalopolis on the California coast; made up of the names Santa Barbara, Los Angeles, and San Diego (194)

savanna (sə van′ ə), a flat grassland (59)

schooner (skün′ ėr), a type of ship with two or more masts; a term sometimes applied to a covered wagon (106)

Schuylkill (skül′ kil), a river in southeastern Pennsylvania. It meets the Delaware River at Philadelphia. (280)

Scioto (sī ō′ tō), a river in Ohio; Circleville is located on the Scioto (27)

Sierra Nevada (sē er′ ə·nə väd′ ə), a mountain range in eastern California (186)

smog (smog), a mixture of fog and smoke (256)

Spokane (spō kan′), a city in eastern Washington (134)

Staten Island (stat′ n), an island lying between Long Island and New Jersey, forming Richmond, one of New York City's five boroughs (125)

stela (stel′ ə), a stone pillar marked with an inscription and used as a monument or a marker (54)

steppe (step), a dry, short-grass plain (88)

suburb (sub′ urb), a residential

area outside a city or large town (149)

Taghaza (täg häz′ ə), a salt-mining center of the ancient Mali Empire (87)
Takedda (tä kā′ də), a copper-mining center of the ancient Mali Empire (87)
Tassili-n-Ajjer (täs ē′ lē·n·ā′ jėr), the site of an ancient settlement in the Sahara; rock drawings have been preserved there (91)
Thames (temz), a river in southern England; London is located on the Thames (98)
Tikal (tē käl′), the site of an ancient Mayan settlement on the Yucatan Peninsula in Mexico (35)
Timbuktu (tim buk tü′), an ancient city in western Africa, once the seat of the Mali Empire (87)
tortilla (tôr tē′ yä), a flat corn-cake used as bread in Mexico since ancient times (51)
tributary (trib′ ü ter ē), a river or stream that flows into a larger river or stream (71)
Tripoli (tri′ pə lē), one of the two capitals of Libya, on the Mediterranean coast of North Africa (93)
Tuat (tü ät′), a city of northern Africa; a major caravan stop in ancient times (89)
tun (tün), a Mayan unit of time, equal to 360 days (48)
tundra (tun′ drə), a treeless, arctic plain (190)

Tunis (tü′ nis), a northern African city on the Mediterranean, now the capital of Tunisia (93)

uinal (wē′ nəl), a Mayan unit of time equal to 20 days (48)

Valparaiso (val pə rī′ zō), a city in northern Indiana, named for a city in Chile (250)

wadi (wä′ dē), a stream bed that fills with water only during the rainy season (89)
Walata (wä lä′ tə), a settlement in western Africa; a caravan stop in ancient times (88)
Wangara (wang gär′ ə), a gold-mining center of the ancient Mali Empire (87)
Worcester (wus′ tər), a city in central Massachusetts (132)

Yaxchilan (yäsk chē län′), an ancient Mayan settlement, probably on the Yucatan Peninsula (46)
Yucatan (u kə tan′), a peninsula in southern North America, extending into the Gulf of Mexico (35)

Zambezi (zam bē′ zē), a river in southern Africa, which flows through Rhodesia to the Indian Ocean (58)
Zimbabwe (zim bäb′ wā), the site of an ancient African settlement in Rhodesia (58)

INDEX

A

adobe, 53
Ahaggar Mountains, 86
airplanes, 23, 35, 115, 119, 178,
   188, 190
   route map, *23*
Algiers, 93
Arabian Sea, 71
Arctic
   Circle, 190
   Ocean, 184
Arkansas River, 109
assembly line, 210–211, 218
Atlanta, Georgia, 182–183
   map, *179*

B

Baltimore, Maryland, 105, 116
   map, *105*
Bangor, Maine, 180–181
   map, *179*
Blair, Nebraska, 185
Bogota, Colombia, 192
Bosnywash, 193, 194
Boston, Massachusetts, 104, 193
   map, *104*
bridges, 101, 102

Buffalo, New York, 121
Buggyaut, 201
buildings
   in the C.B.D., 135, 141–145
   in Chicago, 118
   in the hinterlands, 170
   in modern cities, 21, 133, 249,
      274, 286–289, 292
   in Mohenjo-daro, 71, 72, 79–
      81
   in New York, 125, 290–291
   at oases, 90
   test, 34
   in Tikal, 38–41, 51, 52, 53, 57
   in Zimbabwe, 60–61, 65, 68–
      69

C

cable cars, 139
Cairo, Egypt, 84, 86, 87, 91, 93
calendars, 48
camels, 91
canals, 121
   Erie Canal, 127–128
canoes, 95
caravans, 84–91, 93
Caribbean Sea, 35

cars, 21, 23, 115, 170, 176, 177, 190, 196–222, 261–262

central business district (C.B.D.), 133, 134, 135–147, 149, 152, 153, 154, 166, 168, 217

central city, 131, 132, 140, 153, 168, 221

ceremonies
  in Tikal, 52–53
  in Zimbabwe, 66

Charleston, South Carolina, 104
  map, *104*

Cherry Creek, Colorado, 110, 112

Chicago, Illinois, 107, 116–122, 139, 143, 229, 253–255
  maps, *107, 116, 254, 255*

Chocolate Town, 192

Cincinnati, Ohio, 107
  map, *107*

Circleville, Ohio, 27–31, 32
  maps, *27, 29, 30–31*

city feelings, 2–18, 137, 146–147

city planning, 272–294

city sites, 96–97

city symbols, 20–26, 46, 131, 133, 168

city tests, 32–34
  building test, 34
  food test, 33
  government test, 34
  science test, 34
  size test, 32

trade test, 33

work test, 33

writing tests, 34

Cleveland, Ohio, 235

coasts, 174, 180, 193, 194

Connecticut River, 236–239
  map, *238*

Cornelia, Georgia, 183

Council Bluffs, Iowa, 108
  map, *108*

D

Delaware River, 280

density, 148, 150–151

Denver, Colorado, 107, 108–115
  maps, *107, 108*

deserts, 88, 89, 91, 94, 106, 107, 168, 174, 186

Detroit, Michigan, 201

E

East River, 126

Egypt, 20

Electrobat, 201

elevators, 144–145

estuaries, 105

F

Fall Line, 182

farming
  food test, 33
  in Georgia, 183
  in Hawaii, 189

in the hinterlands, 175
in Maine, 180
in Mohenjo-daro, 74
in Nebraska, 185
in the Owens Valley, 187
in the Rocky Mountains, 112–113
in Tikal, 51
Father Avendano, 5, 57
ferries, 101, 102
flivver, 213
Ford, Henry, 199–201, 207–211
Fords, 101, 102

G

Gao, 87
Garden City, New York, 219
geographers, 97
glaciers, 180
glyphs, 46, 47, 48
"Go-Backs," 111
gold mining
in Denver, 108–112
in Zimbabwe, 66
government
test, 34
Great Lakes, 120, 121, 127, 128
Lake Erie, 128, 232–235
map, *232*
Lake Michigan, 117, 120
Great Plains, 184
Guatemala, 35
Gulf of Mexico, 184
map, *35*

H

hajj, 87, 88, 91, 92
Hallidie, Andrew, 139
Hartford, Connecticut, *21*
Hershey, Pennsylvania, 192
highways, 122, 184, 196, 214, 221–222
Himalayas, 70, 71, 73
hinterlands, 168–194, 229
map, *173*
Honolulu, Hawaii, 188–189
map, *179*
horsecars, 138
Hudson River, 126, 128

I

Illinois River, 121
India, 70
Indian mounds, 27–29, 32
Indus River, 71, 73, 74
Islam, 87, 91

J

jaguar, *36*, 49, 55
in Mayan art, *39*, *49*, *55*
Jefferson, Thomas, 283, 284
Jenne, 87
Jenney, William, 143

K

Kahana, Hawaii, 189
Kansas City, Kansas, 219
Kansas City, Missouri, 107
map, *107*
Kansas River, 109

L

Lake Arrowhead, California, 260–261
map, *260*
Landsberg, Dr. H. E., 248
La Porte, Indiana, 250–255
map, *250*
Limpopo River, 58, 59
London, England, 98–99, 100, 105
map, *98*
London Bridge, 98, 99
Long Island Sound, 238
Los Angeles, California, 186–187, 194, 256–258, 260
maps, *179, 256*

M

Mali, 86, 87, 92, 93
map, *86*
Mambo, 65, 66
Mandingo people, 86
Mansa Musa, 85, 86, 88, 90, 91, 92
Mayas, 37, 43, 44, 45, 48, 49–53, 72, 266
Mecca, 87, 91
megalopolis, 193–194
maps, *193, 194*
Milan, Italy, *24*
mining
in cities, 263–265, 280
in Mali, 85, 87
in the Rocky Mountains, 108–112
in Zimbabwe, 66

Mississippi River, 109, 111, 120, 121, 153, 162, 165
map, *120, 162*
Missouri River, 109
Mobile, Alabama, 104
map, *120*
Model T, 207–209, 210, 211, 212–213
Mohammed, 91
Mohawk Valley, 127, 128
Mohenjo-daro, 70–82
maps, *70, 80*
Monomatapa, 65
Moscow, U.S.S.R., *24*
mosque, 87
Mount Everest, 70

N

New Orleans, Louisiana, *35*
New York, New York, 123–128, 145, 153, 290–291
map, *123*
Niani, 87, 88
Niger River, 87, 93, 95, 96
Nome, Alaska, 190–191
map, *179*
North Pole, 184
numbers
population, 149
in Tikal, 43–45

O

Oahu, Hawaii, 188
oases, 89–90

Oklahoma City, Oklahoma, 276–278

Omaha, Nebraska, 107, 184–185
map, *107, 179*

Owens Valley, California, 186–187

P

Pakistan, 71, 74

paper, 266–268, 270

Paris, France, 102
map, *102*

parking, 217–219
garages, 198, 214, 217
lots, 197, 198, 214, 217
meters, 196

Paterson, New Jersey, 152, 154,
map, *154*

peninsulas, 35, 104, 181

Penn, William, 279, 280, 281, 282

Philadelphia, Pennsylvania, 105, 279–282
map, *105*

Phoenix, Arizona, 151
map, *151*

Piedmont, 182

Pigeon Hill, Maine, 181

Piggly Wiggly, 218

Pike's Peak, 108, 109, 110, 112
map, *108*

plains, 71, 73, 88, 91, 175, 184

plateaus, 91, 182

pollution
air, 242–243, 249, 253–255, 256–262, 272, 282
water, 232–239

population, 148–151
of Mohenjo-daro, 79
size test, 32
of Tulsa, Oklahoma, 246–247

Portland, Oregon, 152, 153, 158, 161
map, *158*

Potomac River, 283

prairies, 106, 107, 109, 114

prairie schooner, 106

Pullman, George, 118

R

rain forest, 36

recycling, 269–270

Red River, 109

Richmond, Virginia, 140

Rocky Mountains, 110, 112, 114
map, *114*

Rozwi, 65, 66, 67, 72

S

Sahara, 89, 91, 96

St. Lawrence Seaway, 122

St. Louis, Missouri, 152, 153, 162
map, *162*

Salt Lake City, Utah, 107
map, *107*

Sandspit, Alaska, 191

San Francisco, California, 104, 139, 151
maps, *104, 151*

Sanlosdiego, 194
Santa Barbara, California, 194
savanna, 36, 59, 60, 61, 68
Schuylkill, 280
science
  in Mohenjo-daro, 78
  test, 34
  in Tikal, 48
Seattle, Washington, 104
  map, *104*
ships, 102, 103, 119, 121, 125–
  128, 188, 281
shopping centers, 197, 198, 219
  Country Club Plaza, 219
  Roosevelt Field, 219
Sierra Nevadas, 186
sites, 96, 97, 100, 101, 102, 103,
  104–105, 107
skyscrapers, 142–143
South Bend, Indiana, 250, 251,
  252, 255
  map, *250*
South Platte River, 110
specialists, 33, 210
  work test, 33
Spokane, Washington, 134
  map, *134*
Sprague, Frank, 140
statues
  in Mohenjo-daro, 76
  in Zimbabwe, 67–69
steam
  car, *203, 262*
  engine, 200

steel frame buildings, 143
stelae, *45, 48, 54, 57*
steppes, 88
streetcars, 138–140, 197, 201,
  216
suburbs, 131, 132, 140, 149, 152,
  153, 162, 166, 168
supermarkets, 218, 219
swamps, 190

T

Taghaza, 87, 93
Takedda, 87
Tassili-n-Ajjer, 91
Thames River, 98
Tikal, 35–57, 72, 166
  map, *35*
Timbuktu, 87, 92–94, 95, 96, 266
Tin Lizzie, 212–213, 214, 219
trade
  in London, 98–99
  in Mohenjo-daro, 77
  in New York, 127
  in port cities, 102, 103
  test, 33
  in Timbuktu, 93, 95
    map, *23*
  in Zimbabwe, 66
trains, 21, 22, 23, 114, 115, 119,
  184, 197, 215, 262
transportation
  airplanes, 23, 35, 115, 119,
    178, 188, 190
    map, *23*

buses, 21
cable cars, 139
canoes, 95
cars, 21, 23, 115, 170, 176, 177, 190, 196–222, 261–262
caravans, 84–91, 93
highways, 22, 184, 196, 214, 221–222
horsecars, 138
ships, 102, 103, 119–121, 125–128, 188, 281
stagecoaches, 113
streetcars, 138–140, 197, 201, 216
trains, 21, 22, 23, 114, 115, 119, 184, 197, 215, 262
maps, *115, 122*
trolley cars, 140
trucks, 22, 23, 119, 190
wagons, 109, 111, 136, 137, 177, 197, 200, 215
tributaries, 71, 73
Tripoli, 93
trolley car, 140
truck, 22, 23, 119, 190
Tuat, 89, 91
Tulsa, Oklahoma, 244–249
map, *244*
tundra, 190–191
Tunis, 93

U

University City, 162, 164, map, *162*

V

Valparaiso, Indiana, 250, 251, 252, 255
map, *250*
volcanoes, 188

W

wagons, 109, 111, 136, 137, 177, 197, 200, 215
Walata, 88, 89
walls
in Circleville, 27–29, 31, 32
in old cities, 25–26
in Zimbabwe, 60, 61, 62–64
Wangara, 87
Washington, D.C., 193, 283–285
Washington, George, 283, 284
Worcester, Massachusetts, 132
writing
in Egypt, *20*
in Mohenjo-daro, 78
test, 34
in Tikal, 42–47

Y

Yaxchilan, 47
Yucatan Peninsula, 35, 36, 37

Z

Zambezi River, 58, 59
Zimbabwe, 58–69, 72
map, *58*

Photo Credits

Art Credits